2614

Liberation,
Revolution, and
Freedom THEOLOGICAL
PERSPECTIVES

Liberation,
Revolution, and
Freedom THEOLOGICAL
PERSPECTIVES

PROCEEDINGS OF THE COLLEGE THEOLOGY SOCIETY

edited by Thomas M. McFadden

ST. JOSEPH'S UNIVERSITY
3 9353 00289 8227

BT
83.57
C6
1974
.C64
1975

A Crossroad Book THE SEABURY PRESS · NEW YORK

005119

The Seabury Press
815 Second Avenue
New York, N.Y. 10017

Copyright © 1975 by The Seabury Press, Inc.
Designed by Carol Basen
Printed in the United States of America

All rights reserved. No part of this book may be reproduced in any form, except for brief reviews, without the written permission of the publisher.

Library of Congress Cataloging in Publication Data

College Theology Society.
    Liberation, revolution, and freedom.

    "A Crossroad book."
    "The essays included here were, with one exception, delivered at the 1974 convention of the College Theology Society at the University of Dayton."
    1. Liberation theology—Addresses, essays, lectures. 2. Violence—Moral and religious aspects—Addresses, essays, lectures. I. McFadden, Thomas M., ed. II. Title.
BT83.57.C64 1975   261.8′3   74–28391
ISBN 0–8164–0271–X

Contents

Introduction

No issue in the past few years has secured for itself such broad and consistent theological attention as the meaning of liberation. Books and articles on the topic abound, and only the rumor of God's demise in the 1960's seems to have occasioned as many Sunday sermons. Yet reactions have been far from uniform. Liberation theology has been hailed as an absolutely essential switch from a theological method heavy with theoretical conceptualizations to one properly consistent with a contemporary emphasis on truth discovered through action. Conversely, liberation theology has been damned as a sell-out of perennial Christian principles in a frantic attempt for acceptance in the name of relevance.

This book presents the mature reflection of several theologians on this topic. Most of the essays adopt a highly favorable attitude, but a few are critical and all point out specifications and/or questions which liberation theology must address if it is to remain a central dimension of Christian thought. What is presented, therefore, is a compendium on the fundamental meaning of liberation theology and its connection with classical Christian values (Part I); its application to the significant freedom movements in America today—the black, Third World, women's, and American Indian liberation movements (Part II); an inquiry into the meaning of violence and Christian attitudes toward it (Part III); and finally several criticisms of the linkage between Christianity and "liberation" (Part IV).

All essays included here were, with one exception, delivered at the 1974 convention of the College Theology Society at the University of Dayton. The task of selecting these thirteen manuscripts was wisely carried out by Rev. William Cenkner, O.P., of The Catholic University of America, and Rev. Thomas Sheridan, S.J., of St. Peter's College, who together with the editor form the Society's editorial board. Their guidance and informed judgments have been invaluable. As a publication of the College Theology Society, the book also reflects the leadership of the Society's national officers: Rev. Matthew C. Kohmescher, S.M., of the University of Dayton, President; Sr. Maura Campbell, O.P., of Caldwell College, Vice-President; Sr. Miriam Ward, R.S.M., of Trinity College (Burlington), Secretary; and Dr. Thomas Ryan of St. Joseph's College (Philadelphia), Treasurer.

The editor would also like to acknowledge with gratitude his children, Monica and David, who have been for him a growing source of the hope in human existence upon which so much of liberation theology is founded.

Thomas M. McFadden
ST. JOSEPH'S COLLEGE
PHILADELPHIA

Liberation,

Revolution, and

Freedom THEOLOGICAL
PERSPECTIVES

I HUMAN LIBERATION AND CHRISTIAN THEOLOGY

Political Theology and Liberation Theology: an inquiry into their fundamental meaning

FRANCIS P. FIORENZA

American theology has always had a precarious relation to its European counterpart. Although American theologians have always sought to work out a theology indigenous to their own national experience and cultural situation, American theology has always had a derivative character. Puritanism, romanticism, Americanism, the social gospel, and even the "death of God" theology have been significantly shaped by European thought. This process has been true for Catholicism even in most recent times, especially with the arrival of transcendental philosophy and theology of the Maréchal school. Lonergan, Coreth, and Rahner have influenced the method and content of American Catholic theology to a degree no American philosopher or theologian has ever done.

Although this process seems to have abated recently, we are now witnessing two new imports: political theology from Germany and liberation theology from Latin America. The re-issuing of hardbacks in paperbacks, the titles of conferences and cassettes, and the announcements of additional translations indicate that the international trade in political

theology and liberation theology is flourishing. Although
both movements are similar to American attempts to
develop a Black theology of liberation[1] and a feminist
theology,[2] the extent of their adaptation in this country has
been a surprise. Yet detractors have not been wanting, and
the protests against political theology and liberation theology have been many and varied. John H. Yoder labels them
fads, but suggests that we can learn from their errors by
observing the narrowness of their selection of biblical
images, the inadequacy of their theological methodologies,
and the ideological configuration of their theology as a new
form of cultural colonialism.[3] Andrew Greeley is incredu-
lous of Metz's rejoinder that political theology has nothing
to do, for instance, with delivering Chicago's electoral
precincts. As a social scientist Greeley feels obligated to
point out that both political and liberation theology lack
even the minimal sophistication of the social sciences;
oblivious of the skills necessary for governing society and
ignorant of the complexity of issues, they are self-assured in
their confidence and speak as if infallible.[4] Richard Neu-
haus warns that Gutierrez ultimately does equate the
mission of the church with revolutionary struggle.[5] And
finally, Stanley Hauerwas claims that political theology
"lumps all issues together under the rubric of the rich
against the poor," refuses to make "discriminating judgments," declines to ask for the ethical justification of a
decision, and places political questions outside the framework of rational discussion.[6] These criticisms are massive, so
massive that one wonders how any intelligent person or
decent theologian could possibly advocate a political or
liberation theology.

The severity of these strictures mandate a closer examination of just what political theology and liberation theology
are about. What are their starting-points as well as their
goals, their presuppositions as well as their methods, and
their achievements as well as their intentions? Are they

guilty of the assumptions and blunders spelled out in the above criticisms? Is there any difference between liberation theology and political theology? Would such a difference be significant for drawing the contours of each in the light of the above criticisms?

In this essay I will attempt to show that political theology and liberation theology represent distinctly different attempts to work out the relation between faith and praxis, religion and society. As representative of political theology I shall consider the work of Johann Metz, Jürgen Moltmann, and Dorothee Sölle.[7] For liberation theology, Gustavo Gutierrez, Juan Luis Segundo, Leonardo Boff, Hugo Assmann, and to a lesser extent Rubem Alves will be studied.[8]

In general the difference between political theology and liberation theology can be drawn fairly sharply. Political theology is a reaction to the consequences of the enlightenment and secularization as they have been spelled out in existential, personalistic, and some strains of transcendental theology. It seeks to overcome the relegation of faith to the private individualistic sphere by elaborating a new hermeneutic of the relationship between theory and praxis. Its primary task is hermeneutical. Liberation theology arises as a response to the oppression and injustices within the Latin American scene. It criticizes the theories of developmentalism and points out the inadequacies of the models of Catholic liberalism as well as the theology of social action or the lay apostolate. Its primary task involves the elucidation of the meaning of the symbols of the Christian faith for the concrete situation and praxis in Latin America.

To elaborate this distinction, I should like to illustrate how each theology interprets the human situation, criticizes previous theological models and offers positive and constructive proposals.

Political Theology

The influence of secularization upon man's understanding of God and society: At the base of political theology is the assumption that the modern world has become secularized, and that a significant change in man's understanding of himself and this world has taken place in modern times. This change, characterized as secularization, is often expressed by the various political theologians as the humanization of the world, the absence of a starting point in man or nature for our knowledge of God, and the destruction of direct religious certainty in the wake of Western European enlightenment. This cultural shift, however, is not negatively evaluated but seen as a positive and new challenge to religion, a challenge to rethink the locus of man's experience of God.

When discussing the relation between faith and the world, Johann Metz asserts that our present historical situation evidences a process of secularization, a transition "from a divinized to a humanized world." [9] Secularization then, is a shift from an emphasis upon the world as natural, numinous, and theophantic to an emphasis upon its historical and anthropological dimensions. The world no longer reveals *vestigia Dei*, but only *vestigia hominis*. Metz finds the phrase, "God is dead" appropriate to the extent that the world is no longer experienced as numinous but has become an object of human subjectivity.

Many of Metz's statements appear to excessively oppose man and nature, partially because they were written prior to current ecological awareness. His emphasis upon human subjectivity, however, points to the history of emancipation and freedom, a history demanding freedom from political as well as ecclesiastic authorities, from tradition as well as ideology. In this context the church is experiencing a crisis not only of its authority, but also of its tradition and metaphysical foundations. Yet this situation of hominization with its resultant emphasis upon freedom, pluralism, and emancipation does not so much present a threat to theology as a challenge. It is this challenge that political theology seeks to meet. It seeks to develop a new context for the experience of transcendence and to articulate the relation of theory to practice in our pluralistic situation.

Jürgen Moltmann also picks up the phrase "the death of God" and calls it an appropriate designation of the modern experience of reality.[10] It expresses what lies at the basis of the modern scientific method and at the foundation of the modern experience of self, history, and the world. God is no longer known from the cosmos, from human existence or from history. In statements reminiscent of early dialectical theology, Moltmann asserts that this experience of the absence of God from our world, existence, and history is where the essential message of Christianity can be most readily heard, where the proclamation of the resurrection of Jesus can become most meaningful. If the resurrection of Jesus is interpreted within the framework of the question of historical probability, of the meaning of existence, or of the validity of church existence, and if the question which the resurrection answers is as broad as the modern experience of God's absence from self, history, and the world, then the resurrection has meaning for all reality by manifesting the transcendent presence of God. The cross and resurrection of Jesus stand in a relation of "dialectical identity" to one another, a dialectical identity of the absence and presence of God. The contradiction and opposition between death and resurrection find their unity in the identity of Jesus. Moreover, Moltmann claims that what happened to Jesus reveals the dialectic of all reality. God's resurrection of Jesus manifests his victory over death. The same dialectic is operative in our present situation. The experience of the absence of God is the other side of the coin of God's revelation of the world's eschatological future in the resurrection of Jesus. This resurrection becomes the foundation of the church's mission and its eschatological hope for the world. It is necessary therefore to establish a theology that takes this dialectic seriously and puts it into praxis, that is a theology that puts its faith and hope in the future of Christ for the world.

Dorothee Sölle also has a similar reference to the slogan "God is dead." [11] For her it expresses the notion that the Western European enlightenment has destroyed the self-evidence of God's existence. God is no longer necessary as a working hypothesis for morality, politics, and science. Although society has taken over many functions of the theistic God through technology and rationalization, this substitution for God is incomplete and unable to satisfy man's religious desire for meaning, purpose, and personal identity. In this situation, Sölle suggests Jesus "represents" God. He is not a God-substitute nor does he replace him, but as both identical and non-identical with God he represents him. Sölle explains that for Christ to represent God is for him "to assume responsibility for the irreplaceable identity of others so that it remains possible for them to attain identity" and "to run ahead to men—before God has reached them, but in order that he may reach them." [12] Moreover, each Christian must in Christ's name take on this representative task. The nature of this task calls for a political theology.

Critique of existential theology: In addition to their common starting-point, i.e., the secularization, pluralism, and anthropocentricity of the modern world, Metz, Moltmann and Sölle also agree that the response of existential and personalistic theology is inadequate, and thereby criticize the dominant strains of twentieth century theology. This criticism is considered a primary task of political theology.

Metz asserts that political theology should first be understood as a "critical correction of present-day theology," [13] necessitated by an erroneous reaction to the enlightenment. The enlightenment shattered the unity of religion and society and reduced Christianity to a particular phenomenon within a pluralistic milieu. Existential and personalistic theology accepted the legitimacy of that separation, and considered the social dimension of the Christian message to be of secondary importance. These theologies privatized the message and reduced the practice of the faith to individual decision, private virtue, or apolitical I-Thou encounters.

Metz insists this response does not meet the challenge of the enlightenment at all. It does not seek to articulate the relation between faith and society under the conditions of contemporary life. Instead the problem is evaded. Faith and social praxis, religion and society, are isolated from one another. This separation surprises Metz since its proponents (especially Bultmann) should have been led by their use of form criticism in biblical research to a similar emphasis on the social, public and communal nature of the gospel message today.[14]

Metz's assertion that "the deprivatizing of theology is the primary critical task of political theology"[15] indicates a fundamental characteristic of political theology. Thus "political" is contrasted with private and individual, and is nearly equivalent to social or public. Ultimately the term political is used, rather than social or public, because today's treatment of the social dimension necessarily includes the political.

Moltmann takes the same point of departure as Metz. However, he broadens Metz's position by analyzing modern society more extensively. Not only is the old harmony between church and society destroyed in modern society, but the very organization of this society differs. Following Hegel's analysis, Moltmann asserts that society is organized around the satisfaction of man's needs by the division of labor. In this society questions of religion are relegated to individual subjectivity and religion is no longer a public duty but rather a voluntary and private activity. The rise of the revivalist and pietist movement alongside of and within the emergence of industrial society has even furthered the emphasis upon pious individualism and the religious withdrawal from social goals.[16] A theology of transcendental subjectivity does not meet the challenge of the situation but only confirms the withdrawal of religion from societal life. The same tendency is at work in an ecclesiology where the "true" church is pitted against the institutional church and is understood as a purely spiritual entity, a community of pure happening. Here the church is described as a nonworldly phenomenon that is diametrically opposed to the state. In such an understanding, a model of disengagement (*Entlastung*) is implied. But whereas this ecclesiology seeks to disengage any Constantinian symbiosis between religion and politics, it overlooks that in practice such a disengagement is itself highly political. This approach implicitly sanctions a positivistic rationality and thus regards the end as independent of the means.

In contrast, the model of correspondence attempts to apply paradigms from the realm of the church and faith to political life. Although this model acknowledges the difference between the dynamics of faith and politics, and thereby refrains from an arrogant presumptuousness toward political life, it does articulate categories of correspondence "from above" and thus often remains abstract and idealized.[17] Moltmann seeks, therefore, an approach that would comprehend "God in the world, transcendence within immanence, the universal in the concrete, and the eschatological in history so as to arrive at a political hermeneutic of the crucified and a theology of real liberations." [18]

Whereas Metz and Moltmann directly criticize the existential reduction of religious faith in Bultmann's theology, Sölle picks up Metz's insight that form criticism should have led Bultmann to elucidate the public character of the Gospel. She argues that form criticism and historical criticism find their logical consequence not in existential interpretation, but in political theology. Thus she argues with Bultmann against Bultmann.[19] According to Sölle, the historical criticism adopted by Bultmann is a sociology of knowledge. In regard to the gospels, historical criticism sought the social conditions in which oral traditions were preserved or forgotten. It investigated the cognitive interests and structures that played a role in the formation of the Christian tradition. It revealed that the Gospel pericopes were transmitted by a community as public sermons, and that they addressed the interests of the community. Thus the gospels have a political and not merely a private significance, and a political interpretation of the Christian message is not antithetical to Bultmann's theology but is instead its logical consequence.

Sölle also capitalizes on Bultmann's insistence upon textual relevance. According to Bultmann, if a text does not add something to one's self-understanding, if a text does not say anything to question one's security, then the text basically has no authority. But where Bultmann judges the authority of a text by its capacity to address a concrete situation at the time it was written, Sölle extends this authority and relational truth to our *present* concrete situation and its political questions. Bultmann's stress upon the authority of the text and its right to question our self-understanding does not, then, offer a basis for an apolitical interpretation, although this may be what Bultmann does when, for example, he interprets Romans 14:7 ("The reign of God is . . . righteousness and peace . . .") as referring to the peace of the individual. Against such *de facto* interpretations, Sölle proposes that political theology has essentially a hermeneutical function.

Political hermeneutics: In addition to characterizing the present as secularized and criticizing existential and personal theology, political theologians also define theology as primarily hermeneutic, i.e., as centrally concerned with the methodological principles functional in any contemporary

interpretation of the Christian message. The positive task of
political theology, Metz asserts, is to determine anew the
relation between religion and society, specifically under the
conditions of modern society. This task involves a problem
different from the traditional one of determining the
relation between historical and systematic theology. Instead, political theology is concerned with the relation
between theory and praxis, between religion and society.[20]

This hermeneutic is outlined by Metz in the form of
imperative suggestions. First, the biblical eschatological
promise includes images of liberty, peace, justice, and
reconciliation. These images are necessarily public. An
interpretation of these images in an individualistic or
privatized sense does not do justice to them. Secondly, the
eschatological character of these images prevents any
equation between the total realization of these images and
any specific society or political order. This eschatological
awareness, moreover, should be the driving force behind
every political theology insofar as its task is to point out the
provisional character of every state, party, or societal
condition. Political theology must articulate faith, hope,
and love in such a way that love for example is not seen
primarily as interpersonal, but as social in its resolve to
work for justice and peace. At the same time, political
theology points out that the complete fulfillment of its
resolve is eschatological.[21]

In order to take the pluralism of modern society seriously
and to avoid relapsing into a Constantinian model of
political theology, Metz also suggests that political theology
must "assert its essentially universal categories as a negative
critique in this society." [22] The notion of critical negation is
crucial for Metz. He believes that through negation the
church can achieve a larger consensus within a pluralistic
society, and yet perform a positive function through this
negation. For example, Christians might not have had a
positive solution to the Vietnam war but they might have

protested earlier against the inhumanity and immorality of certain military measures used during that war.

In his more recent writings Metz has added some corrective motifs. In contrast to his previous emphasis upon the newness of the future, he has begun to emphasize the necessity of remembering the passion, death, and resurrection of Jesus.[23] This memory of the crucified Jesus reveals the contrast between eschatology and teleological progress.

Although Metz makes several suggestions about the significance of suffering within a political hermeneutic, that subject is central to Moltmann's political theology. Moltmann agrees that every eschatological theology must become a political theology, and regards the latter as fundamental hermeneutical norm for the whole of Christian theology.[24] The key to his hermeneutic, Moltmann asserts, is found within the Pauline combination of a theology of the cross with eschatological hope. Paul emphasizes the "not-yet-ness" of Christian salvation against the realized eschatology of his enthusiastic opponents by pointing out how essential an element the cross is to Christian life.

The theology of the cross is used by Moltmann as the hermeneutical principle in criticizing every political, theological, and societal idolatry.[25] Because political theology is based upon a theology of the cross, it can no longer be used to justify a political situation, but only to criticize such justifications. Such a political theology moreover, not only rejects any identifications of religion and politics, but also criticizes the theological images operative in such identifications. Moltmann criticizes traditional theism for making impassability a central attribute of God rather than taking the cross seriously. He suggests a new trinitarian understanding of God which not only allows but also demands that God Himself suffer.[26] In this suffering of God Moltmann sees the meaning of the crucifixion of Jesus and attempts to develop a response to the question of theodicy. Finally, Moltmann explains how a political hermeneutic should not only be concerned with the critique of political religion and with the revision of theological tradition, but also with the distortions of human life in the present, especially the vicious circles of poverty, violence, industrial exploitation of nature, racist and cultural alienation.[27]

Echoing many of the same themes as Metz and Moltmann, Sölle argues that political theology has been incorrectly understood as a theological solution to properly political and social questions, or a defense for a Constantinian church-state linkage. She prefers the expressions "political interpretation" or "policial hermeneutics" in order to avoid such caricatures.[28] Political theology does not attempt to develop a concrete political program from faith nor does it seek to work out a social gospel in which social practice absorbs all theory. Although political theology does in specific cases have concrete application, it should be understood in a broader sense and not as an exchange of traditional content for that of the political sciences. The Christian faith does not have specific and ready-made answers for concrete and complex problems of our situation today.

Political theology as a theological hermeneutic does not interpret reality from an ontological or existential horizon, but rather sees politics as the decisive sphere for the praxis of Christian truth.[29] Existential theology asks "What meaning does this Gospel text have for my individual life?" Political theology asks, "What is the meaning of the Gospel text for the life of all men, not for the individual person alone but for the life of every one, for the society of persons that constitute the whole world?" Such an horizon allows theology to take much more seriously the cosmological dimensions of the New Testament's eschatology and allows political theology to transcend Bultmann's demythologization of New Testament eschatology. Such an interpretation also enables theology to grasp the social nature of sin and to see the importance of political as well as individual forgiveness. For Sölle, it is important to observe that a correct political hermeneutic does not seek to ask whether Jesus was a revolutionary, a socialist, or had an explicit critique of societal structures. This procedure would be ahistorical and fundamentalistic. Yet it is important to analyze the implications and consequences of Jesus' preaching and action even if they are only indirect.

In short, if we look at these three political theologians, it is quite evident that they agree on three basic points. The contemporary situation is secularized, the existential response is inadequate, and a political theology is not a theology of politics, but a hermeneutical task that has its place in fundamental theology.

Latin American Liberation Theology

Latin American theologians[30] live and think in a very different context. Their theological opponents are not European existentialists and their constructive proposals do not center on hermeneutics.

Secularization, not construed as an absence of the experience of God but as the commitment of the Church, is a central theme of the Latin American scene.[31] The difference between European and Latin American culture, moreover, forms the basis of a major objection leveled against political theology by liberation theologians. Gutierrez points out[32] that even though Metz reacts against any peaceful coexistence between an individualistic faith and a secularized society, he nevertheless operates within the parameters of a theology of secularization when he assumes that the world is universally secularized and faith is everywhere privatized. He transfers what perhaps describes the European scene to the world at large. The cultural differences of places like Latin America are not noticed or taken into account.

The faith and the Church still have a public dimension in

Latin America. Although the situation is changing insofar as the Church is becoming more critical of the political order, the Church still plays an important role in confirming and supporting the established government. Metz's "privatization of faith" oversimplifies the problem and does not correspond to the Latin American situation.[33] The question in Latin America, where the Church still has great influence, is primarily concerned with the uses of this influence. At a time when Latin America is rapidly becoming more industrialized the question of secularization has a special urgency if Latin America is to avoid the patterns of Europe and the United States.

Juan Luis Segundo suggests in *Our Idea of God*, the second of a five volume series on systematic theology for adult education use,[34] that Latin America has its own special destiny to proclaim a new understanding of the Christian tradition and of western civilization.[35] Since Christianity and western civilization have so mutually conditioned one another and become so intertwined, a crisis for one necessarily involves a crisis for the other. Where the aggressiveness and rapaciousness of western civilization has become so brutally evident as in Latin America, a crisis arises not only for western culture but also for the Christian faith in God. The situation of Latin America differs from that of Europe because Latin America experiences exploitation much more directly and immediately. On the other hand, since Latin America exists on the periphery of the western industrialized society where secularization has not yet become as advanced as in Europe, the Church and Christianity have much more influence. The oppression and exploitation in Latin America, consequently, present themselves as challenges for the Church to become committed to serving society, rather than isolating itself from society.

Segundo proposes that the cultural difference between Latin America and Europe can be illustrated by contrasting the "death of God" theology and the Latin American understanding of secularization. Although theologians often use the labels "death of God" and "secularization" to refer to a similar cultural process, they are quite distinct.[36] Among the affluent the sacred and the secular are separate, the religious element within society is eroded, and the Church is isolated from the world. Such a cultural situation, characteristic of the West, is aptly described by the epitaph, "God is dead." In Latin America, poverty and exploitation have led to the Church's involvement with society, as the documents of the Second General Conference of the Latin American Episcopate at Medellín show when they reveal the Church involvement in liberation. They show a consecration of the Church to the profane and they acknowledge that the service of humanity is a place of encounter between God and man.

Critique of developmentalism and Catholic liberal social action movements: A second common strain running through all liberation theology is the criticism of developmentalism as well as Catholic liberalism.[37] The demand for liberation arose in Latin America during the early 1960s as a reaction to developmentalism, i.e., the attempt to achieve social advances within existing structures and without altering these structures. Developmentalism originally referred only to economic achievement and industrial growth, but was broadened to include cultural and social progress as well. As such it ran into strong criticism, and failed to show any substantial progress. The cause of this failure was attributed to developmentalism itself, since it left intact the power groups and international interests that were at the heart of the problem.

The bishops at Medellín described various attitudes toward societal and political change.[38] Three groups are delineated: the traditionalists who lack social consciousness and are interested in the preservation of privileges and the established order; the developmentalists or evolutionists who seek to expand the means of production and are more interested in economic improvement than social progress; the revolutionary groups who seek a change of goals as well as means and, although they agree on radical change, vary as to their ideologies and approaches.[39]

The bishops criticize the last group's exclusive identification of the faith with political and social responsibility. But in the document on peace, the bishops denounce the extreme inequality among social classes, the exploitive use of power by groups unjustly insensitive to the misery of oppressed persons, the international system of dependency and its distortion of trade, and those unjust situations that constitute institutionalized violence.[40] The bishops demand liberation from cultural and social obstacles to humanization. Liberation is negatively described as the elimination of oppressive human relations, structures, and systems. It encompasses not only biological and economic but also cultural and social spheres. The positive understanding of liberation is elucidated in the document on education. Influenced by the theories of Paulo Freire,[41] the bishops postulate a liberating purpose for education. Education should not adapt persons to existing structures, but make them aware of their fatalistic and fearful attitudes toward the world. It should enable persons to become subjects of their own self-determination so that they can help in their own transformation as well as in the transformation of the dominant social and economic structures. The bishops assert this liberating education to be a part of the Church's mission because "all liberation is an anticipation of the complete redemption of Christ." [42] They explain that human values have a supernatural dimension, belong within the economy of salvation and converge in Christ.

These episcopal statements reveal why liberation theology criticizes and replaces the notion of development. Liberation has a comprehensive and inclusive meaning that contrasts sharply with the single dimension of developmental theories. This integral comprehensiveness of liberation is most clearly elucidated by Gustavo Gutierrez and his three levels or dimensions of liberation.[43] On the level of scientific rationality liberation is primarily understood as economic, social, and political change. On the level of utopian imagination, liberation involves historical projections for the creation of a new man and a new social solidarity. Finally, on the level of faith, liberation is freedom from sin and communion with God and all men. All three levels belong integrally connected.

Parallel to the critique of developmentalism is the criticism of Catholic liberalism. Although Catholic liberalism sought to overcome the Constantinian model of the Church-world relation, it did so by means of a distinction of planes.[44] The hierarchy, usually identified with the Church itself, was responsible for the supernatural and religious dimensions of life, whereas the layman was obligated to care for the world. He did so not so much on the basis of his Christian faith as on the basis of a general and universal ethic. This approach had the same effect as developmentalism. Insofar as the Church was limited to a purely religious role and the layman was involved in the political order only as an individual but not as a Christian, the political structures with their injustices are left unchanged and unchallenged.

Liberation and the symbols of Christian faith: Where political theology concentrates upon the proper hermeneutic, liberation theology is concerned with interpretations of the Christian symbols of faith. It is less concerned with the question of whether or how these symbols can be significant, and attempts to look at them from a liberationist perspective.

Thus Segundo points out that the Trinitarian debates in early Christian times are not merely speculative controversies but imply a "political theology"[45] insofar as man's conception of God determines our understanding of God's relation to the world.[46] Both Modalism and Sabellianism reduced the Christian idea of God to an abstract deity of Greek culture. God manifests himself in Jesus but essentially remains separate from him and our human world. In Subordinationism and in Arianism the same isolation between God and the world is effected because the Son is a being inferior to God. Only the Trinitarian understanding of God affirms the radical presence of God in Jesus and in human history. Only then are we freed from our perishable human natures. Segundo points out that the Roman emperors exploited monotheism in the interests of political unity and for the sake of securing their position. The early Christian Church, however, withstood this manipulation insofar as it elaborated a fully developed Trinitarianism.[47]

Segundo suggests that a Trinitarian understanding of God must be reaffirmed and reappropriated today, that it can be a critical and liberating image for Latin America.[48] Appealing to the imagery of the "Merciful Trinity," a formula originating in France around 500 A.D., Segundo opts for a social rather than psychological understanding of the Trinity. This formula confesses that the three persons are equal in divinity and "concordant by virtue of Trinity." Where we would expect "concordant in spite of their Trinity," the formula entails the unity of being and action as a result of the love among the three. In the face of all the twisted and distorted images that human beings have of themselves and society, the Christian tradition offers an understanding of God as a God of love who is a society of love. This image is in no way ideological (against the Marxists of Latin America), and is a liberating force for understanding ourselves and society.[49]

Leonardo Boff offers a similar Christology from a liberationist perspective. In *Jesus Cristo Liberatador*,[50] a best-seller in Brazil, Boff attempts to analyze the Gospel tradition as well as the Chalcedonian formulas of faith. Along with other liberation theologians, Boff does not identify Jesus with the Zealots or make him into a revolutionary. He is quite conscious of recent exegetical research on the relation between the historical Jesus and the kerygmatic Christ, and he recognizes that Jesus's preaching and activity contain only an implicit Christology. Boff argues, however, that Christ's preaching and activity can best be represented by the explicit Christological title of liberator. Jesus is understood as liberating persons from human restrictions (the law, human conventions, and authoritarianism), from powers that alienate human beings (sin, demons, sickness), and even from the total alienation of death. The Chalcedonian formulas do not imply that human nature is an instrument of the divine person, but that Jesus is fully human in the perfect way that God alone could realize.

At the center of all the deliberations by the liberation theologians stands the question of the Church and its mission. Here Gutierrez, Segundo, and Boff[51] take as their starting-point Rahner's conception of the Church as a sign of universal salvation. This idea has been adopted by Vatican II and involves an "uncentering" of the Church. The Church is not the sole place of salvation but only the sign of salvation. The church can be understood only in reference to God's universal salvational will, the action of Christ and his Spirit in history. The Church realizes its mission insofar as it signifies and proclaims that salvation. The Eucharistic celebration commemorates both the salvific action of Christ in history and signifies the creation of human brotherhood. As a meal, it is a sign of community and brotherhood, as a passover meal it recalls the political liberation of Israel, and as a memorial of Christ's death and resurrection it commemorates man's liberation from sin. When the Church combines its celebration with the creation of brotherhood, it gives witness to what it signifies. Its confrontation with the oppression and injustice of its concrete situation is an integral part of its mission to be the sign of salvation.[52]

Conclusion: Political Theology or Liberation Theology?

Our survey indicates the contrast between political and liberation theology. Political theology takes as its starting-point the secularization and pluralism of modern society, criticizes the response of existential theology to this situation, and proclaims itself a hermeneutic endeavor. Liberation theology is aware of the oppression and injustice within the Latin American situation; it appeals to the Church to further the radical change and transformation of persons and societal structures, and it justifies this involvement in terms of the meaning of the Christian symbols of faith and the nature of the Church.

In light of this difference we can understand the main point of controversy between liberation and political theology, involving the relation between theory and practice, and the role of ethical reflection in mediating between theory and practice. Political theologians, especially Metz, insist upon the mediating role of a political ethics, i.e., the autonomous process (distinct from specifically theological reflection) of deciding upon moral issues in the political sphere. Liberation theologians reject such a mediation, and Hugo Assmann criticizes Metz for this emphasis on political ethics.[53] Gutierrez not only refers to Assman's criticism of Metz on this point, but he also objects to Catholic liberalism for this reason.[54] Gutierrez thinks that the emphasis upon political ethics grants the world too much autonomy from the Christian faith and leaves the Christian with nothing to say to the world. These points, however, need to be examined more closely since they seem to be based on a misunderstanding of the relation between theory and praxis.

Both Moltmann[55] and Metz reject any direct and immediate politicization of eschatology, just as Sölle criticizes the notion that the Christian faith has ready-made answers to concrete problems. In Metz's opinion, political theology moves toward action only indirectly and mediately through political ethics.[56] This mediation of political ethics is important for it avoids the danger of absolutizing political measures, as if there were an immediate transition from Christian faith into action, and properly regards the transcendent character of eschatology. All of history stands under the eschatological judgment of God and no immediate political program or party can ever be exempt from this judgment. Furthermore, the complexity and pluralism of modern society demands such an ethical mediation. Such an ethics, however, is not independent of the Christian faith as a rationalistic understanding of ethics would have it. One of the prime tasks for political theology is to work out precisely the relation between the Christian vision of faith and ethical theory and praxis. These explicit reservations against an immediate transposition of faith into practice show that the critics cited at the beginning of this essay misunderstand the fundamental intent of political theology when they accuse it of absolutizing judgments and refusing to make discriminating ethical and societal judgments.

But does liberation theology fall under that verdict? Gutierrez points out "to assert that there is a direct, immediate relationship between faith and political action encourages one to seek from faith norms and criteria for particular political actions." [57] Any assertion that faith and political action have nothing to do with each other places them on distinct and unrelated planes. But Gutierrez also points out the danger of a politico-religious messianism that fails to respect the autonomy of the political. He suggests that if faith is to develop norms and criteria for political options, it can do so only on the basis of a rational analysis of reality and through the mediation of a utopian ideal of what man should be. Although Gutierrez does not appeal to a political ethics as does Metz he appeals to rational analysis and utopian vision which together would mediate between faith and praxis.

A more detailed analysis of Gutierrez's suggested mediation between theory and praxis is impossible here, yet it is clear to what extent the critics have also misunderstood liberation theology. As a matter of fact, much of liberation theology's criticism of political theology, Alves's critique of Moltmann for example, is based upon a desire for more concrete historical and societal analysis.[58] In this sense liberation theology sees more clearly than political theology the conflicts and antagonism of the present societal structures and is therefore more of political theology than public theology.

I should like to suggest, therefore, that the North American situation requires both political and liberation theology. In the United States the hermeneutical function of political theology can only be achieved when political theology becomes liberation theology.[59] Similarly, the liberating function of liberation theology can only be effected when liberation theology also takes up a hermeneutical task. Our situation is neither the secularized situation claimed for Germany (whether this claim is true of Germany is another question), nor does our Church have the same direct influence as in Latin America. Instead we face three possible "religious" attitudes: a civil religion, an invisible religion, and a sectarian version of Christianity. What is meant by the American civil religion, the linkage between Christianity and Americanism, is evident from inaugural addresses of our Presidents,[60] and also from our "holy wars" and identification of our political enemies with the enemies of God. What has been termed "invisible religion," [61] can be viewed less as a secularization of religion than as a canonization and sacralization of individualistic and private attitudes. Since its major themes and emphases are individualistic rather than social or political, invisible religion becomes an implicit sanction of the status quo. Finally, the United States has a long history of sectarianism, be it religious or secular, that has been more often than not a Christianity of withdrawal rather than of involvement. It has emphasized devotion over action, love over justice, individual conviction over social critique. It has often criticized the political involvement of Christianity but in an inconsistent manner. Roger Shinn says, "For example, the critic of political theology may appeal to the authority of Jesus in a highly selective way, invoking that authority at those points where it separates God and Caesar, but neglecting it where it tells of the involvement of God with men or the clash between God and Caesar." [62] Against these religious attitudes, a political hermeneutic must be developed. It must not be limited to a prolegomena to theology, but extend to all the symbols of Christian faith, observing their use in history and in our present society. Only then will theology become liberated.

Notes

1. See James H. Cone's essay in this volume as well as his *Black Theology and Black Power* (New York: The Seabury Press, 1969) and *A Black Theology of Liberation* (New York: J. B. Lippincott Company, 1970). See also Deotis Roberts, *Liberation and Reconciliation* (Philadelphia: Westminster Press, 1971); John S. Mbiti, *African Religions and Philosophy* (New York: Doubleday, 1969); and Gayraud Wilmore, *Black Religion and Black Radicalism* (New York: Doubleday, 1972).

2. Rosemary Ruether, *Liberation Theology* (New York: Paulist Press, 1972). This work also contains an analysis of Latin American liberation theology.

3. "Exodus and Exile: The Two Faces of Liberation," *Cross Currents* 23 (1973), pp. 297–309.

4. "Theological Table-Talk: Politics and Political Theologians," *Theology Today* 30 (1974), pp. 391–397.

5. "Liberation Theology and the Captivities of Jesus," *Worldview* 16 (1973), pp. 41–48.

6. "Politics, Vision, and the Common Good," *Cross Currents* 20 (1970), pp. 399–414. Although he grants that not everyone

advocating a political theology has all these faults, he lists Metz, Moltmann, and Herzog as the main proponents of a political theology.

7. I am limiting myself mainly to German political theology and Latin American liberation theology. For a comparison between Black theology and the political theology represented by Moltmann, cf. G. Clarke Chapman, Jr., "Black Theology and Theology of Hope: What Have They to Say to Each Other?" *Union Seminary Quarterly Review* 29 (1974), pp. 107–129; and also "American Theology in Black: James H. Cone," *Cross Currents* 22 (1972), pp. 139–157.

8. For a survey of literature and a list of bibliographies on Latin American liberation theology, cf. Francis P. Fiorenza, "Latin American Liberation Theology," *Interpretation* 28 (1974).

9. *Theology of the World* (New York: Herder and Herder, 1969). For a comprehensive bibliography, an analysis of political theology, and a reply from Metz, see Helmut Peukert, ed., *Diskussion zur 'politischen Theologie'* (Munich: Chr. Kaiser Verlag, 1969). See also Francis P. Fiorenza, "The Thought of J. B. Metz: Origin, Positions, Development," *Philosophy Today* 10 (1966), pp. 247–252.

10. *Theology of Hope*, trans. by James W. Leitch, (New York: Harper and Row, 1967), pp. 165–203. Cf. Francis P. Fiorenza, "Dialectical Theology and Hope, I" *Heythrop Journal* 9 (1968), pp. 143–163.

11. *Christ the Representative: An Essay in Theology after the 'Death of God,'* trans. David Lewis (London: SCM, 1967).

12. *Ibid.*, p. 114.

13. *Op. cit.*, p. 107.

14. *Ibid.*, pp. 108–111.

15. *Ibid.*, p. 110.

16. *Op. cit.*, pp. 304–338.

17. *Der Gekreuzigte Gott* (Munich: Chr. Kaiser Verlag, 1972), pp. 293–315.

18. *Ibid.*, p. 297.

19. *Political Theology*, trans. by John Shelley (Philadelphia: Fortress Press, 1974). The German original had the subtitle, "Confrontation with Rudolf Bultmann."

20. *Op. cit.*, pp. 108–124.

21. "Political Theology" in *Sacramentum Mundi*, volume 5, (New York: Herder and Herder, 1970), pp. 34–38.

22. *Ibid.*, p. 37.

23. "Kirchliche Autorität in Anspruch der Freiheits-geschichte," in *Kirche im Prozess der Aufklärung*, by J. B. Metz, J. Moltmann, and W. Oelmüller (Munich, Chr. Kaiser Verlag, 1970), pp. 53–90; and "The Future *Ex Memoria Passionis*," *Concilium* 76 (1972), pp. 9–25; and "A Short Apology of Narrative," *Concilium* 77 (1973), pp. 84–96; and "Erlösung und Emanzipation," *Stimmen der Zeit* 98 (1973), pp. 171–185.

24. "Theologische Kritik der politischen Religion," in *Kirchliche, op. cit.*, pp. 11–51.

25. *Umkehr zur Zukunft* (Munich: Chr. Kaiser Verlag, 1970), pp. 168–197.

26. *Der Gekreuzigte, op. cit.*, pp. 184–267.

27. *Ibid.*, pp. 306–308.

28. *Political, op. cit.*, pp. 55–69.

29. *Ibid.*, pp. 71–92.

30. For a general survey, cf. Philip E. Berryman, "Latin American Liberation Theology," *Theological Studies* 34 (1973), pp. 357–395; Hans-Jüurgen Prien, "Liberation and Development in Latin America," *Lutheran World* 20 (1973), pp. 114–132.

31. For the situation in Latin America, see Gary MacEoin, *Latin America: The Eleventh Hour* (New York: P. J. Kennedy, 1962) and *Revolution Next Door: Latin America in the 1970s* (New York: Holt, Rinehart and Winston, 1971); Thomas C. Bruneau, *The Political Transformation of the Brazilian Catholic Church* (London: Cambridge University Press, 1974); Guenther Lewy, *Religion and Revolution* (New York: Oxford University Press, 1974), pp. 504–536.

32. *A Theology of Liberation*, trans. by Caridad Inda and John Eagleson (Maryknoll, New York: Orbis Books, 1973), pp. 220–225.

33. *Ibid.*, p. 224.

34. The series, translated by John Drury, is being published by Maryknoll in New York. The following have appeared: *The Community Called Church, Grace and the Human Condition, Our Idea of God,* and *The Sacraments Today.*

35. *Ibid.*, pp. 34ff.

36. *Ibid.*, pp. 74–99.

37. Gustavo Gutierrez, "Liberation and Development," *Cross Currents* 21 (1971), pp. 243–256. The critique of developmentalism in no way implies for Gutierrez and others that to eliminate external dependency necessarily and immediately leads to full liberation.

38. For the official English translations, see *The Church in the Present-Day Transformation of Latin America*, vols. I and II, edited by Louis Michael Colonnese (Bogota, General Secretariat of Celam, 1970).

39. *Ibid.*, 7, 5–11.

40. *Ibid.*, 2, 2–16.

41. *Pedagogy of the Oppressed*, trans. by Myra Bergman Ramos (New York: Seabury Press, 1970).

42. *The Church, op. cit.*, 4, 9 and 1, 3.

43. *A Theology, op. cit.*, pp. 232–239.

44. *Ibid.*, pp. 63–77.

45. *Our Idea of God, op. cit.*, p. 73.

46. *Ibid.*, pp. 98–177.

47. Julio Vidaurrazaga, "La Trinidad: problema politico" *Mensaje* 176 (1969), pp. 27–30.

48. Segundo develops aspects which Erik Peterson's classic essay neglected. See "Der Monotheism as politisches Problem," in *Theologische Traktate* (Munich: Kösel, 1951), pp. 45–147.

49. Segundo, *Idea of God, op. cit.*, pp. 64–66. See Denzinger 17.

50. (Petropolis, Brazil, 1972). A response to critics and the tenth chapter is reprinted in *Revista eclesiastica Brasileira* 32 (1972), pp. 515–539, which is edited by Boff.

51. *Die Kirche als Sakrament im Horizont der Welterfahrung* (Paderborn: Verlag Bonafacius-Druckerei, 1972). This was his doctoral dissertation at the University of Munich. Pages 499–537 give Boff's own systematic attempt to work out the significance of church as a sign for the Latin American situation. See also Gutierrez, *A Theology, op. cit.*, pp. 255–285 and Segundo, *A Community, op. cit.*, pp. 3–49.

52. Gutierrez, *A Theology, op. cit.*

53. "Teología política," *Perspectivas para el Dialogo* 50 (1970), p. 307.

54. *A Theology, op. cit.*, pp. 53–61, 64–77, and 220–250.

55. "Hope and the Biomedical Future of Man," in *Hope and the Future of Man*, edited Ewert H. Cousins (Philadelphia: Fortress Press, 1972), pp. 89–109.

56. " 'Politische Theologie' in der Diskussion" in Peukert, *op. cit.*, pp. 279–296.

57. Gutierrez, *A Theology, op. cit.*, p. 236.

58. Ruben A. Alves, *A Theology of Human Hope* (New York: World, 1969), pp. 55–68.

59. This has been done most appropriately by Frederick Herzog in "Political Theology in the American Context," *Theological Markings* 1:1 (Spring 1971), pp. 28–42; J. Robert Nelson, John Deschner, and Frederick Herzog, "A Discussion about Political Theology," *Theological Markings* 3:1 (Spring 1973), pp. 21–34, and Herzog's most recent book, *Liberation Theology* (New York: The Seabury Press, 1972).

60. Robert Bellah, *Beyond Belief* (New York: Harper and Row, 1970), pp. 168–189.

61. Thomas Luckmann, *The Invisible Religion* (New York: Macmillan Co. 1967), pp. 69–114.

62. Roger L. Shinn, "Political Theology in the Crossfire," *Journal of Current Social Issues* 102 (Spring 1972), pp. 10–20, esp. p. 15. Shinn's article is one of the most perceptive and balanced articles on the problems and issues of political theology.

Freedom as Personal and Public Liberation

MARY I. BUCKLEY

A crucial problem for Christianity today is to combine genuine personal commitment to the liberation given in Jesus Christ with that same liberation in its world-wide dimension, especially through structural social change.

At first sight it may appear that the Christian faith is concerned only with the individual. Alfred North Whitehead wrote that religion is "what the individual does with his own solitariness." [1] Rudolf Bultmann in a commentary on Romans 14:17 spoke of God's kingdom as concerned basically with the bliss of the individual.[2] It would seem that only persons can be converted, yet recently Helmut Thielicke wrote an article asking, "Can Structures Be Converted?" [3] An emphasis on the individual and his desire for salvation leaves us uneasy as we reflect on our world today, a world more structured and organized than any man has known. Today, the individual appears encircled and smothered by fate. He can only lift a threatening fist in powerlessness against the mighty structures that encompass him, withdraw into his private shell, or fit into the 'system' unquestioningly. Genuine freedom appears illusory and fate becomes overwhelming.

Therefore, if the commitment to personal liberation as

well as to structural social change is to remain integral, man
cannot be understood in isolation. No man is an island. He
is neither the detached observer of history nor the sole agent
of history. He is, from the first, related to a community, to
others, to the world, to nature. He is embedded in social
and cultural relationships. Communication with the world
around him is underway at every moment; reflection and
action form one movement. Transformation of the world
and transformation of the individual go hand in hand and
the first is no simple addendum to, no mere consequence of,
the second. The experience of the twentieth century has
made this clear in a new way as men recognize that mass
hunger, world-wide air, land and water pollution, and the
spread of themonuclear weapons affects the liberation of
everyone. The realization is growing that "we are all under
the ax. All of us are likely to be doomed or saved
together." [4]

In the paper, *Justice in the World*, the Roman Catholic
Bishops' Synod of 1971 emphasized this relation of man to
his world, stating, "Action on behalf of justice and participation in the transformation of the world fully appear to us
as a constitutive dimension of the preaching of the Gospel,
or in other words of the Church's mission for the redemption of the human race and its liberation from every
oppressive situation." [5] Christian social action is accordingly not a mere sequitur to personal faith commitment. It
is a constitutive part of that commitment from the outset.
Reflection on this leads to a renewed understanding of faith
within a political and personal context.

But it is not easy to grasp the dialectic at work between
these two commitments. Generally speaking, it is easier to
focus on one or the other. In the past three centuries,
Western Christianity has emphasized the personal element
of faith.[6] It is also possible to center on society and its
structures, so that the individual is regarded as determined
by forces beyond his control. Yet the two commitments

belong together. It appears to be the task of our time to probe their inner relationship as was not possible when theology was held within the categories of the Hellenistic metaphysical tradition. The emergence of "this-worldly" emancipation movements are significant here.

The Emancipation Movements

The two main emancipation movements of contemporary times can be subsumed under the labels of liberal humanism and Marxist humanism. An overall theme for them is found in Jean Jacques Rousseau's famous phrase, "Man is born free, and everywhere he is in chains." [7] Rousseau spoke of men in the midst of their concrete historical situation and asked how the chains could be broken since freedom must at least begin in this world.

Liberal humanism is associated with the French and American revolutions, and with the cry of "freedom, equality and fraternity." It stresses the importance of the individual, his liberties, rights and duties. The signs of this humanism are evident in such documents as the American Bill of Rights, the United Nations Declaration of Human Rights, the recent Humanist Manifesto II. [8]

Marxist humanism emphasizes the need for the liberation of all men everywhere. This humanism points to the social context, the social relationships in which men find themselves enchained. Marx delineated structures of power which upheld particular class interests and were therefore structures of oppression. Liberation within the Marxist analysis requires the dismantling of the unjust structures in society which hold men down. [9]

These two important emancipation movements direct men's attention to this world, to concrete political rights, and to the oppression found in economic, political and cultural orders. Their main proponents rejected the established Christian religions, labeling their tutelage a tyranny, and the Christian God, a tyrant. The aspects of truth in their accusations are today accepted by many Christians. The established churches had become hardened and were often a barrier to scientific, historical and political freedoms. They appeared to close off new possibilities in the name of a redemption to be found in the "other world" or one dependent on an older cultural embodiment (the Ancien Regime).[10]

But an important tension exists between these two humanisms. Marx accused liberal humanism, which is concerned with individual rights and liberties, of a bourgeois, elitist mentality.[11] Although he affirmed the rights that the liberals championed, he said they remained abstract because they dealt with man individualistically and were unrelated to the social context. Marx regarded the civil rights of the liberals as rights for the upper middle class only; the great masses of people had little possibility of claiming these rights because unjust social structures barred them from breaking through to liberation. Only with basic revolutionary changes in the structures of society would individual freedom obtain a wider base. So great a change could not be wrought by a stress on abstract ideals alone. Only active engagement with the concrete situations could bring about effective change. This "theory-praxis" or understanding of truth is different from what prevails in Greek and idealistic thought. Truth is not so much something which is "there" and needs only to be discovered by the observer from the reality before him. It is rather a knowledge gained only by living and doing in the concrete reality of the world. The new becomes possible only within history.[12]

The Marxist awareness of the oppressive structures is shared by many. For example, Pope Paul VI wrote in April 1972 to the Secretary General of the United Nations Conference on Trade and Development, "You are aware that neither the reform of international trade nor the improvement of aid and co-operation are capable of themselves of ensuring a more united and more human development among peoples. In many cases it is the very structures of power and decision-making that must be altered. . . . Does not justice demand that all peoples, whatever their degree of economic power, should have a real participation in all negotiations of world-wide importance?" [13]

Marx's emphasis on the relation of theory and practice, reflection and action, parallels the biblical approach to truth as something lived, practiced, created. To theology it offers a new hermeneutic.[14] It is by doing the will of God, that we will know. Living faith is not merely an assent to propositions; it is an integral combination of faith and love. Truth is realized in the concrete reality of society, including from the first the public as well as the personal dimension.

The analysis of structures and the affirmation of theory-praxis are illuminating aspects of the Marxist position and a valid criticism of liberal humanism. These two points are also of great value for a new interpretation of theology, even though this political/personal interpretation of theology has its own difficulties. Its critical task of de-privatizing theology is in general acceptable; its constructive task has only just begun.[15]

Meanwhile we can ask of both emancipation movements some critical questions. Both movements are centered in this world and seek man's liberation in the midst of history. At the time of the French Revolution and throughout the nineteenth century, a great élan carried Western man along in the hope for progress and for a world of harmony and peace ushered in by man himself. A great optimism was evident, man was thought of as perfectible and evil as conquerable in the not too distant future.[16] Today no one is optimistic in this way. On may sides we hear of limits to growth,[17] of the tremendous population explosion, of the multitudes who may die from hunger in the next decade,[18] of wars and rumors of wars. A new realization of the immense weight of evil, almost a sense of doomsday, is present in the modern world. Personal and collective guilt pervades society.[19] I recognize that I enjoy steak, coffee, and tea at the expense of the poor and ragged in other lands. The affluent societies are affluent not on their own, but because others have been milked and exploited.[20] Gradually too, I recognize that I cannot live in peace in the midst of such injustice; my own luxury turns against me and makes life meaningless.[21] The optimism of the emancipation which ultimately affirms that freedom can be achieved by new arrangements of laws and structures somehow rings hollow. We find ourselves trapped if man must depend on himself alone to achieve a new creation and a new world.

This sense of confinement within a closed and often ugly world raises in a new way the question of grace, of gift. Is man alone, or is his liberation finally something that comes to him from another, from the one man calls God? Is genuine hope possible even in the midst of catastrophe? And even if men should find brotherhood and newness, what about all the centuries of men who have endured in slavery and hunger, in torture and disfigurement? What is the meaning of life for all human beings, both past and present? With an awareness of our great problems today the question of transcendence and of God is posed anew.

Christian Freedom Today

Emancipation and Christian freedom—at first sight these two seem alien to each other. Men threw off the shackles of the Christian churches and the Christian God in search of a wider freedom for men, a worldy freedom made by themselves. Yet one thing must be noted. Despite inquisitions and actual historical resistance, there is a deep relationship between the emancipation movements and Christian faith itself. As Jacques Maritain, who was not friendly to emancipation movements, wrote long ago, the living aspects of Christian faith, rooted ultimately in the Gospel, could find an outlet into the world only through the seemingly hostile movements of emancipation.[22] Christopher Dawson went so far as to say that Marx spoke like the Hebrew prophets "of the Day of the Lord, in which the rich and powerful of the earth should be consumed and the princes of the Gentiles brought low, and the poor and the disinherited should reign in a regenerated universe." [23] The search for the new creation and the new man which had been too etherealized broke out anew in secularized form.

As Christians today review the past three hundred years, we have learned much from the emancipation movements. We have learned that salvation is intimately linked to liberation in this world, even as it also transcends this world. Christians are the "strugglers" who are not called out of the world but called into it as cooperators with God and with each other for their own individual transformation as well as the world's transformation. The way back to God is through man and the world.

Christians have also learned that social structures and personal life are enmeshed, both for good and for evil. Technological developments have forced us to look in this direction, and the Marxist analysis has been invaluable. The conviction that society can be transformed cannot be abandoned in favor of a privatized Christianity, nor can it be abandoned despite the failure or success encountered. As Ernst Käsemann, the biblical exegete, has written, ". . . the gospel has to do not only with the individual person's belief or unbelief, but with world history." [24] Jesus is the Lord of the earth as well as the Lord of individual hearts.

But what can this renewed understanding of Christian faith bring to modern men who find themselves enchained anew, even by the very discoveries which seem to promise greater freedom? How does the freedom which Jesus Christ came to bring relate to the concrete historical life of man? This question goes deep, especially in the light of evil, oppression, crisis and doom that is present in modern society. Contrary to the optimism of earlier decades, a deep pessimism regarding man's future is present on a wide scale; some see that future as containing diminished freedom on every side.[25]

Yet the whole of the New Testament speaks of freedom:[26] "for you were called to freedom, brethren . . .",[27] says Paul, and again he speaks of the "glorious freedom of the children of God." [28] Christians speak of Jesus Christ as the Savior of mankind, as the one who has come to set men free, to liberate from every bond that oppresses, to bring men to a hitherto unknown and richer life. This Christian faith can have meaning for men today, revealing to them a dimension of liberation which they desperately need but cannot achieve for themselves. We can approach this affirmation in two ways: first, by disclosing man's great need for deliverance from the inner and outer evils that oppress him, from the evil done by himself and the larger, structural evil in which he is a collaborator; and secondly by revealing man's longing for a better life, for his own transformation and the transformation of his world—a hope that does not finish with death but looks out beyond history.

Liberation from Moral Evil, Personal and Collective

The force of evil weighs heavily on men today. Man, the only reflective one among the animals, the only one who knows he will die, can kill not merely for food but for revenge and with malice. As we look out into the world, we see structures of evil, structures of injustice. Just as slavery was an unjust structure, so too are the mighty structures of monopoly capitalism oppressive to men today.[29] On the smaller, familial and neighborhood levels there are oppressive microstructures. In this framework, evil is more readily traceable to individual guilt. Yet actions which were meant well often go awry and the reason for evil or malice escapes our full comprehension. True freedom seeks to conquer this moral evil. The great emancipation movements hoped for this, but it is clear that man cannot do this for himself. To paraphrase St. Paul, "the good that I will I do not, the evil that I will not, that I do." It is true that neither any religion nor any philosophy can fully explain the mystery of evil,[30] but Christian faith can give men eyes to see the depths of evil as well as courage to repent and the ability to begin anew. Faith speaks of the forgiveness of sins, the conversion of the heart which comes to man through other men and ultimately from God. As Dorothee Sölle has written, ". . . there is no argument for forgiveness of sin. . . . What is required is a judgment in favor of the guilty, an advance of trust in him that establishes the possibility of a new beginning." [31]

The liberation that comes through forgiveness is ultimately a gift. Today we recognize that the forgiveness needed, though it must be always intimately related to the individual, is nevertheless wider in its ambit. Structures of injustice exist which set men at enmity with each other. Insofar as we collaborate with these structures (and the great majority of us do),[32] we are guilty and in need of forgiveness. Responsibility for collective evil cannot be ignored even though any real disentanglement is an overwhelming task.

Hatred, misery, war and famine cannot any longer be laid completely at the door of fate or be blamed upon a few evil men. Men are responsible for their society; genuine reconciliation is possible only where rectification and trust begin. For forgiveness at this level, we need to build new public structures. We should not think of God forgiving, "behind the backs of other men and without the laborious detour through the world . . ." [33] Without community or church structures of authentic forgiveness, the convict or the traitor go through life as the unforgiven ones, as people who do not really belong. Personal and public sin are interwoven; to experience forgiveness we need the trust of other people which is ultimately rooted in a love and forgiveness that dwells among men, but is more than man.

Liberation through God's Rule in History and Transcending History

The positive approach which completes the way of forgiveness discloses the question of hope. How is it possible for man to hope in spite of his sin, but also in spite of his inadequacy and failure? How especially can he hope to change the mighty systems and take part in the building of a better and more human world? The very immensity of these structures today lead us to turn away in resignation. How can we continue to hope even when our best efforts fail and neither ourselves nor the world is transformed? In some sense the essence of Christian faith is a hope that never gives up. Such hope is a gift, like forgiveness. Man receives it, he cannot make it for himself.[34] But this gift does not alienate man like the work of a "deus ex machina" or the patronizing gift of a lady bountiful. Rather it works with man at the heart of his experience and his world, and tells of a God who cares and who dwells with men.

For this hope to be genuine today, it must also take on public form. Men can neither be forgiven nor can they hope in isolation. A community of hope is needed both in the churches and in society at large. It is true of hope as it is of faith that "each man can believe only in solidarity and can be a man of faith only in community." [35]

The Grounds for Hope and Forgiveness

The life and work of Jesus Christ as he walked the roads of Palestine, as he by word and deed touched men's hearts and directed them to help their neighbors and build new forms of human communication, grounds this personal and public liberation of Christian faith. The life and praxis of Jesus led to his death, but God raised him from the dead so that to follow him is the way to life and freedom.[36] This following is no slavish imitation; it is a following that is living and true in the context of a new time and place. The public dimension of freedom is present throughout the Old Testament. The people of Israel are continually reminded to be just and loving to the stranger, the fatherless child, the widow, for "You shall remember that you were a slave in the land of Egypt." [37] Jesus deepens this public dimension as he speaks to persons; without the commitment of the heart there is no real life. This is indispensable and it is ultimately not confined to the individual.[38] We know today that God's promised rule and kingdom are central to the aims of Jesus Christ. A fuller grasp of this message has been one of the fruits of biblical scholarship over the past decades. "Revelation shows us beyond doubt that the New Testament is concerned, not merely with human existence, but at the same time with world history." [39]

Liberation is ultimately grounded in the eschatological dimension of the Good News, in the preaching and promise of God's rule and kingdom. Man is always man in community; God's promise inaugurated in Jesus Christ, touching human life in the present yet reaching out beyond history, means that personal and collective liberation are bound together at the heart of the Christian faith. Salvation is at once intimately personal and eminently social. Liberation is indeed realized by the individual but the individual is from the first related to others and to the world.

At its deepest level this liberation is always a gift, a gift given ever anew, which refuses any categorization of man as finished, completed and without new possibility. It is not a gift that robs man of his part but calls him to be a cooperator with God. That this gift is present in the midst of life cannot ultimately be proved. Its message is carried by the Christian heritage; its verification is not by way of propositions but in the testimony given through Christian life and action.

Notes

1. A. N. Whitehead, *Religion in the Making* (New York: Macmillan, 1926, 1960), p. 16.

2. R. Bultmann, *History and Eschatology: The Presence of Eternity* (New York: Harper Torchbook, 1962), p. 42.

3. H. Thielicke, "Können sich Strukturen Bekehren?" *Zeitschrift für Theologie und Kirche*, 66 (1969), pp. 98–114.

4. J. M. Swomley, Jr., *Liberation Ethics* (New York: Macmillan, 1972), p. 1

5. *Roman Synod: Justice in the World* (Washington, D.C.; U.S. Catholic Conference, 1971). Reprint by Crux Information Service, Albany, N.Y., 1971, p. 1.

6. J. B. Metz, *Theology of the World*, trans. Wm. Glen-Doepel (New York: Herder & Herder, 1969), pp. 107–155. Paul and Arthur Simon, *The Politics of World Hunger* (New York: Harper's Magazine Press, 1973), pp. 214–217.

7. *The Social Contract*, trans. by G. D. H. Cole (New York: E. P. Dutton, 1762, 1913 and 1914), Everyman's Library, p. 5.

8. "Humanist Manifesto II," *The Humanist*, 33, Sept./Oct., 1973, pp. 4f.

9. Erich Fromm, *Marx's Concept of Man* (New York: Frederick Ungar, 1961), p. 25. Marx thought that it might be possible that the U.S. and England could change without revolution.

10. J. B. Metz, J. Moltmann and W. Oelmuller, *Kirche im Prozess der Aufklärung* (Münich: Kaiser Verlag, 1970); L. Gilkey, *Naming the Whirlwind* (Indianapolis: Bobbs-Merrill, 1969), pp. 3–228. A good account of secularization.

11. Karl Marx, *The German Ideology* (New York: International Publishers, 1970), pp. 39–52.

12. Karl Marx and Friedrich Engels, "Theses on Feuerbach," *The German Ideology* plus supplementary texts, *op. cit.*, pp. 121–123. Thesis II: ". . . Man must prove the truth, i.e., the reality and

power, the this-sidedness of his thinking in practice. The dispute over the reality or non-reality of thinking that is isolated from practice is a purely scholastic question."

13. See H. Camara, *Structures of Injustice* (London: Justice and Peace Commission, 1972). Cited on back of second un-numbered page.

14. J. B. Metz, *op. cit.*, p. 112. "Properly speaking, the so-called fundamental hermeneutic problem of theology is not the problem of how systematic theology stands in relation to historical theology, how dogma stands in relation to history, but what is the relation between theory and practice, between understanding the faith and social practice." Cf. J. Moltmann, "Toward a Political Hermeneutic of the Gospel, *Religion, Revolution and the Future*, trans. M. Douglas Meeks (New York: Scribner's, 1969), pp. 83–107.

15. Dorothee Sölle, *Political Theology*, trans. and with an introd. by John Shelley (Philadelphia: Fortress Press, 1974), pp. xii–xiii of the Introduction by J. Shelley.

16. *Man Alone: Alienation in Modern Society*, edited with an introduction by E. and M. Josephson (New York: Dell Publishing Co., 1962). See introduction, especially pp. 19–20.

17. *The Limits to Growth*, A Report for the Club of Rome's Project on the Predicament of Mankind by D. H. Meadows, D. L. Meadows, J. Randers and W. W. Behrens III (New York: New American Library, 1972).

18. Paul and Arthur Simon, *op. cit.*

19. R. Heilbroner, "The Human Prospect," *New York Review of Books*, Vol. 20, Nos. 21 and 22 (January 1974), pp. 21–34. K. Menninger, M.D., *Whatever Became of Sin?* (New York: Hawthorn Books, 1973), especially pp. 94–132. W. G. Pollard, "The Uniqueness of the Earth," *Earth Might Be Fair*, ed. I. G. Barbour (Englewood Cliffs, N.J.: Prentice Hall, 1972), pp. 82–99.

20. Camara, *op. cit.* See also Barbara Ward, *The Angry Seventies* (Rome: Pontifical Commission of Justice and Peace, 1970).

21. Herbert Marcuse, *One-Dimensional Man* (Boston: Beacon Press, 1964).

22. *True Humanism*, trans. M. R. Adamson (London: G. Bles, The Centenary Press, 1938, 1946), pp. xiv–xvii.

23. *Progress and Religion* (New York: Sheed & Ward, 1929, 1934), p. 229.

24. *Jesus Means Freedom*, trans. F. Clarke from 3d revised ed. of 1968 (Philadelphia: Fortress Press, 1970), p. 133.

25. Heilbroner, *op. cit.* He sees the possibility of military rule in many parts of the earth and diminishing freedom.

26. Käsemann, *op. cit.* The whole book centers round the freedom that Jesus brought.

27. Galatians 5:13.

28. Romans 8:21.

29. Camara, *op. cit.* There are many books that could be cited here.

30. F. von Hügel, *Essays and Addresses I* (London: J. M. Dent, 1921, last reprinting 1963), pp. 98–116. A letter to a woman who found it difficult to believe on account of the evil in the world.

31. *Op. cit.*, pp. 98–99.

32. H. Gollwitzer, *The Rich Christians and the Poor Lazarus*, trans. D. Cairns (New York: Macmillan, 1970).

33. Sölle, *op. cit.*, p. 104.

34. H. Kessler, *Erlösung als Befreiung* (Düsseldorf: Patmos Verlag, 1972) p. 124.

35. Francis Fiorenza, "The Security and Insecurity of Faith," a seminar paper, *Proceedings of the Twenty-Eighth Annual Convention of the Catholic Theological Society of America* (Bronx, N.Y.: Manhattan College, 1973), p. 197.

36. Kessler, *op. cit.*, pp. 17–37.

37. Deuteronomy 24:22.

38. R. Schnackenburg, "Die nachösterliche Gemeinde und Jesus," *Die Aktion Jesu und die Re-Aktion der Kirche*, K. Müller, ed. (Würzburg: Echter Verlag, 1972), pp. 140–147.

39. Käsemann, *op. cit.*, p. 133.

Ancient Israelite Laws and Liberation

ELIZABETH BELLEFONTAINE

The earliest period of Israel's history, the so-called settlement period, is described by George Mendenhall as involving a "rejection of control of human beings by force and the proclamation that only God was in control." [1] Our study of the laws will examine this description of ancient Israel during the time of its formation as a people. We hope to demonstrate that the Israelite laws governing festivals, the sabbath, the ownership of land, and attitudes toward the poor were all enacted to combat the slavery, oppression and poverty characteristic of the non-Israelite communities of the time. The Israelite laws provided for the freedom and social equality that form an important basis for human liberation and have contributed to the Christian ideal of liberation.

Mendenhall interprets Joshua 24 as a ceremony of covenantal amalgamation at Shechem by which an incoming group who had experienced the saving event of the Exodus offers faith in Yahweh to disaffected people of Canaan. [2] The latter are exhorted to renounce the worship of their traditional gods and to worship Yahweh alone. The conversion of these indigenous people to Yahwism was preceded by their rejection of the social, political, and religious

principles of the Canaanite feudal order.[3] Mendenhall
interprets the widespread destruction of towns and cities
and the internal chaos reflected in the Amarna letters (the
diplomatic correspondence between Egypt, Mesopotamia,
Syria, and several small vassal states in the 14th century
B.C.) as a social rebellion taking place in Canaan during
the 14th and 13th centuries B.C. It was a "peasants' revolt
against the network of interlocking Canaanite city-states," [4]
a revolt to which the masses were driven by the oppressive
forces of the Canaanite feudal aristocracy. Rejecting Canaanite society and its economic and religious bases, the
disaffected natives found themselves lacking both community and deity. The Yahwist immigrants offered both.
Yahweh, the patron of those Hebrews delivered from
Egyptian bondage, became the hope and source of freedom
for the oppressed people of Canaan.

Accepting this thesis in principle, i.e., that the Yahwist
religion offered a source of liberation to Canaanites reacting
against an oppressive system, we turn to the legal texts of
the Old Testament to consider certain laws of the pre-
monarchic period that are indicative of the social and
religious aspects of Israelite life at that time. I propose that
these ancient Israelite laws be viewed as pronouncements of
freedom rather than constraining legal precepts, and that
they confirm Mendenhall's historical description. While
fundamental expressions of Israel's understanding of its God
and of its relationship to him aimed at maintaining the
sovereignty of Yahweh, I submit that these laws were also
revolutionary measures. They laid the foundations of a way
of life for a society of free and equal members.

The Command to Worship Only Yahweh

The principle commandment of the Israelite covenant
was the command to worship Yahweh alone. At Shechem,
only one stipulation is explicitly stated in the account as it

now stands: the people are commanded to serve the Lord and to "put away" other gods (Joshua 24:14 f., 23) in order to enter into covenant with Yahweh. The meaning is clear: Yahweh demands exclusive service and obedience from his people. The account does not deny the existence of other gods; it emphasizes that those who choose to worship Yahweh must refrain from any kind of service to other gods.

Rolf Knierim convincingly argues that the prohibition against the worship of strange gods was first formulated at Shechem.[5] During their wandering, the Exodus group honored Yahweh as their God, but they had not yet formulated a prohibition against strange gods. The biblical texts which express the prohibition (Exodus 22:19; 23:13; 34:14) all evidence that this originated in the period between the settlement and the establishment of the monarchy. The decalogue command of Exodus 20:2 offers no such evidence, but after a study of the traditions of the wandering in the desert, Knierim concludes there is no basis for positing the drafting of this commandment during the desert period. The express formulation of a prohibition against the worship of strange gods was first necessitated by the merging in Canaan of the various Israelite tribes, by their encounter with Canaanite deities and also, as we have noted above, by the incorporation into the Exodus group of the Canaanite converts.

That this renunciation of alien gods was rooted in the Shechemite cult of ancient Israel is clear from the local traditions of the sanctuary found in Genesis 35:2 and 4. The texts echo the same tradition as Joshua 24 and witness a specific religious practice of the tribal league by which all objects belonging to an alien cult had to be brought forward and ritually buried before the people pledged themselves to worship only Yahweh.[6] Thus, the demand for the exclusive service of Yahweh was the fundamental obligation of the Israelite covenant. It was constitutive of the Israelite federation from its foundation, providing the principle of unity among the members.

In its exclusive worship of one god, Israel stood alone among its neighbours in the ancient Near East. No people save Israel dedicated itself to the worship of a single deity. No god save Yahweh imposed upon his worshippers the intolerant demand for exclusive worship.[7] In Palestine, the Israelites were in direct contact with an elaborate and mighty pantheon of Canaanite gods under whose control all aspects of natural and human life lay. That Yahweh, in the face of such contact, was regarded as the sole object of Israel's worship, is evidence of a religious and social revolution at the very origins of Israel's formation. Any prohibition in Canaan against worship of other gods appears as deliberate polemic against polytheistic cults and a conscious rejection by Israel of the basic structure of Canaanite religion. In a nation where the gods and goddesses provided the theological support of the monarchical feudal system and where the king was both lord and high priest, the renunciation of the religious base of society was a renunciation of society itself. Therefore, while deriving from Israel's experience of its God, this principal covenant commandment also involved a revolutionary break with the whole structure of Canaanite life and an attempt to lay the foundations of a new and better existence.

We will see the social ramifications of such action shortly. On the religious plane, the sole worship of Yahweh held the promise of continued assistance by this God who had revealed himself as the liberator of the enslaved, the champion of the downtrodden. At the same time, it released the people from the burdens of polytheism, from the obligation of having to please and appease numerous deities. It freed them from the fear of overlooking or offending one or other of the deities and so of calling upon themselves divine wrath and revenge. It further liberated them from the insecurity of having to discern the will of these unpredictable and often capricious gods and goddesses. Yahweh, on the other hand, was one God, one who had shown himself both able and willing to save his people. Moreover, in the law he had made his will known to his people and had promised blessings to those who obeyed him.

The Laws Governing Israelite Festivals

Yahweh's blessings were obtained in bountiful harvests and celebrated in the annual religious feasts. The laws pertaining to the feasts are found in the cultic calendars which are included in all the major legal collections (the Book of the Covenant, Exodus 23:10–19; the Yahwist Decalogue, Exodus 34:18–26; the Holiness Code, Leviticus 23:1–44; and the Deuteronomic Code, Deuteronomy 16:1–17). The people are directed to observe three feasts a year by offering the first fruits to Yahweh at his shrine: a feast of Unleavened Bread celebrated in the spring; a harvest festival of the late summer; and a feast of Ingathering celebrated in the fall. It was stipulated that no Israelite was to appear before him empty handed.

The most ancient aspect of these feasts is their agricultural origin. As agrarian feasts they were first celebrated by Israel in the land of Palestine, and must have been borrowed from the Canaanites. In observing them, Israel was not unlike other agrarian societies. Nevertheless, the laws which governed the feasts reveal the intention of the Yahwist religion. Their distinct character is highlighted when contrasted with the religious intent inherent in the Canaanite festivals. From what we know of the Canaanite religion,[8] we can say it was intimately bound up with the cycles of nature. The cultic re-enactment of the myths in which fertility rites played a prominent role was directed toward releasing the divine powers operative within the cycle of nature, thereby insuring the preservation and renewal of the vital processes upon which life was dependent. The dominant concern in the observance of these festivals was the security to be gained through the regular rhythm of nature within which life was maintained and renewed.

It is significant that no aspect of this religious intention is found in the Israelite calendar of feasts. Certainly, the cycle of nature is recognized in the regular celebration of the annual festivals. But there is no effort to identify Yahweh with any of these natural forces, and absolutely no attempt to control life through cultic dramatization of these forces. On the contrary, the absence of these elements is indicative of a tacit but powerful acknowledgement of Yahweh's separation from nature and of his uniqueness. At the same time, by offering joyful thanksgiving at the harvest periods, Israel recognized Yahweh's power over nature and its own dependence upon him for the goods of the earth. In the Israelite festivals, then, the worshipper was freed from the constraint and insecurity inherent in the Canaanite ritual. The fertility of the earth was celebrated as the fulfillment of Yahweh's covenant promise to bless his faithful people, and in the offering of the fruits of the earth, Yahweh's power and will to save are experienced anew.

The Sabbath and Sabbatical Year

Two other observances directly related to Israel's attitude toward the soil, namely the sabbatical year and the sabbath day observances, also reveal a liberating force. The seventh year was a period of rest for the land from all agricultural activity. But this rest is not fully explained by the practical purpose of preserving or increasing productivity.[9] Nor can it be understood as observed out of a subjective fear or awe of the powers of the soil. In Israel the obligation of the fallow was a sacred duty. The prescriptions establishing it (Exodus 23:10–11) form part of the cultic prescriptions regulating the observance of the sabbath day and the annual pilgrimage feasts. The total cessation of the cultivation of the soil was an acknowledgement of Yahweh's sovereignty over the land. In like manner, his sovereignty is affirmed by the cessation of labor, that is, of all agricultural activity, on the sabbath day. The belief expressed in these observances was that the land belonged to Yahweh, and to him it was "returned" by the periodic interruption of cultivation.[10] By formulating and preserving prescriptions which regulated these practices, Israel expressed its understanding that, like a vassal, it held its land only in tenure; rightful ownership belonged to Yahweh.

At the same time, these observances were for the Israelites periods of rest and joyful expressions of freedom. The people of the covenant recognized that their Lord was not like the lords they had worked under in Egypt and Canaan, oppressive masters who allowed no release from their enforced labor, and no break in their constant daily toil.[11] Their God not only permitted but commanded rest from the daily toil of man's occupation. Now as free men, vassals to no human lord and subject to no human force, the Israelites laid down their tools and, like the land, were rested and renewed.

Ownership of Land

The most significant stipulation concerning Israel's attitude toward the land is the precept of Leviticus 25:23 which reads: "The land shall not be sold in perpetuity, for the land is mine." In its present context, the precept forms the basis for the Jubilee Year reversion. Scholars accept, however, that the fundamental concept expressed by the text is of cultic significance in early Israel.[12] According to Numbers 26:52–56, the land was apportioned to the tribes

according to their size and then allotted to clans and
families within the tribes. Two seemingly incompatible
methods of land division are described: one, apportionment
of tribal shares according to the size of the tribes; the other,
distribution by lot-casting. The passage belongs to the
priestly source and cannot be considered historical. Nevertheless, the author evidently felt it necessary to fuse the two
methods of division, indicating he was working with traditional principles which could not be ignored. The situation
recurs in Numbers 33:54. Here, again, the allotting of the
land as an inheritance is performed by the casting of lots
while, at the same time, an adequate relationship between
the size of the tribe and that of the allotted territory is
retained.[13] The principles underlying the two methods of
land division are not difficult to ascertain. In the Old
Testament the casting of lots was a cultic activity used to
ascertain the divine will.[14] Apportioning the land by lot,
therefore, implied Yahweh's sovereignty over the land and
his act of granting it in fief to the members of the tribe or
clan as an inheritance. The insistence on proportionate
allotment to the tribes indicates that, although the area of
tribal territories varied, the portions of the clans and
families within the tribes were to be equal.[15] The principle
of equality is operative as the basis of land ownership in
ancient Israel.[16]

According to Leviticus 25:23 this family and tribal
inheritance which each one held by virtue of his member-
ship in a certain tribe was not to be permanently sold. Such
a provision ensured Yahweh's right of proprietorship over
the land. It prevented the Israelites from exercising a
control over their property which is proper to the owner.
The Israelites were to conduct themselves as vassals with
regard to the land; in no way were they to behave as if they
held title to their fields and vineyards. No Israelite was to
conduct himself as "lord" over his inheritance.

The function of this regulation is, therefore, covenantal

rather than economical. Nevertheless, besides this theological motivation, the prohibition against the alienation of inherited property had the effect of ensuring the preservation of an economic parity of land tenure in Israel. If adhered to, it would prevent the gradual growth of latifundism and the rise of a wealthy landowning aristocracy in control of a large, landless peasantry, a situation which aptly describes the Canaanite structure. Under the Lordship of Yahweh, the Israelite system fostered equality and stability of land tenure.

Such a system of land tenure envisioned a society without social classes. In a world where social structures had direct reference to their respective systems of land ownership, this was revolutionary. In particular, it is remarkable that the social system Israel developed in the midst of Canaan was totally opposed to the Canaanite feudal system with its social stratification based on land tenure. The economic and social equality envisioned by the parity principle of land allotment and strengthened by the prohibition against alienation of property demonstrates that from its origins there was in Israel a conscious effort to withstand the development of a feudal system of land tenure with its accompanying structure of class distinction. Yahweh was Lord of Israel and of each Israelite to whom He entrusted a portion of His land. In no way does He appear as the theological support of a ruling feudal class. Each Israelite was equally a member of the covenant community and entitled to a portion of Yahweh's land.

Protection of the Poor and the Stranger

Despite such efforts toward maintaining equality in the community, certain individuals were reduced to less fortunate circumstances than the rest of their fellow-Israelites. They are referred to in the texts as the "poor" and the "needy," among whom are specified the widow, the orphan, the stranger, and the slave. Such persons, in this early period, did not constitute separate social classes, nor even one class of "poor people" within the society. The poor were individuals, and because of that they were all the more vulnerable.

The earliest prescriptions concerning them are found in Exodus 22:20–23 which reads: "You shall not wrong a stranger. You shall not afflict any widow or orphan." The Hebrew verb translated as "afflict" connotes harsh treatment, oppression, even violence against an indigent group which lacks the power to defend itself (e.g., Genesis 15:13; Exodus 1:11). In particular, the word is used to describe the plight of the Hebrews in Egypt, subject to the oppression of their Egyptian taskmasters, socially weak, and totally defenseless (cf. Genesis 15:13; Exodus 1:11; Deuteronomy 26:6; I Samuel 12:8). In this manner the lot of the widow and orphan is depicted.

In similar straits was the stranger who, for one reason or another, had left his own family and tribe and entrusted himself to the protection of another tribe. As a stranger, he could not share in the inheritance rights of the tribe and so was prevented, at least in this early period,[17] from owning property in Israel. It was his landlessness with its resulting dependency and impoverishment that caused him to be classed with the poor, the widow and the orphan.

The law forbids any affliction or oppression of these unfortunates. Already socially weak members of the community, lacking normal legal protection, they are not to be reduced to even more dependent positions. No advantage is to be taken of them and no more fortunate member of the community is to make himself lord or taskmaster over them. There was to be no oppression by human force in Israel.

In similar vein the law of Exodus 22:25 prohibits the exacting of interest from any poor member of the covenant community. The request for loans was made out of financial desperation. Indebtedness was the principal cause of slavery in ancient Israel.[18] The insolvent debtor was forced to sell himself as a slave in order to pay his debt. An interest rate on loans would have made it more difficult to cancel one's debts and would have led to oppressive and controlling practices against less fortunate Israelites. The stipulation against exacting interest from fellow-Israelites was designed to prevent any further imbalance of the economic difference between the poor and those who were in a position to lend assistance. Beneath this lies a religious demand for social equality among the Israelites, an equality demanded precisely because they are members of the same covenant community.

Indebtedness did, however, force some Israelites to enter the service of their creditors in order to pay off debts. It is this type of slavery for debt which receives limitation in the laws of Exodus 21:2–6 stipulating that a Hebrew slave must be allowed to go free after six years of service. Among all the peoples of the ancient Near East, slaves constituted an accepted strata of society. Not so in Israel. On the contrary, the biblical regulation aims at preventing the rise of such a class by providing special safeguards against exploitation of the poor. It prohibits the permanent enslavement of not just a certain class of Israelites, but of all Israelites. While the enslavement of foreigners was permitted, the permanent enslavement of Israelites by Israelites was strictly forbidden, although a provision was made for the man who at the end of six years voluntarily chose to bind himself for life in the service of his master (Exodus 21:3–6; Deuteronomy 15:16–17). The intent of the provision against permanent slavery is that no Israelite may exploit another or make himself lord over his brother. All Israelites are equally members of the covenant community, and freedom for all must be safeguarded.

Conclusion

From this brief consideration of Israel's laws, we conclude that the Yahwist community designed a revolutionary way of life for itself in Canaan. The only existing political system upon which it could have modelled itself was that of the kingdom in either its grand form as exhibited by the major empires of the time, including Egypt, or in its smaller scale visible all around in the city-states of Canaan. Israel rejected this structure, not only in principle, but also in practice. By refusing to pattern its social and political life on the monarchy, Israel rejected the only political model available to it.

This model had come to mean slavery, oppression and poverty; it meant control by human force legitimized by the support of the gods. Freedom, on the other hand, meant classlessness, self-determination, and personal responsibility to the community. It is not difficult to understand, then, why in Israel the laws governing the relationships of Israelites to the land and to fellow-Israelites reveal a constant effort to initiate and maintain social equality in the covenant community. Freed from the slavery and oppression of a feudal and stratified society, whether Egyptian or Canaanite, the Yahwists snatched the opportunity for freedom and a better way of life. In the laws governing their religious and social institutions, they laid the foundation of a new life of freedom.

However, this life of freedom amounted to more than a political and social revolution. The political and social differences between Canaanites and Israelites were grounded in totally different views of God and his dealings with men. Grounded in the covenantal relationship, the religious and social framework of Israelite community life was directed primarily toward ensuring the sovereignty of Yahweh. Yahweh alone was Lord in Israel and no Israelite was to conduct himself as "lord" over what belonged to

Yahweh by divine right—whether this was His land or His people. It was with this type of community that Yahweh was in covenant. From its origins, Israel understood that Yahweh was Lord, that He was a saving God, and that He wills for his people liberation, justice, and freedom.

Notes

1. George E. Mendenhall, *The Tenth Generation: The Origins of the Biblical Tradition* (Baltimore: The Johns Hopkins University Press, 1973), p. xiii.

2. Although Joshua 24 shows clear signs of redaction, especially by a Deuteronomic hand, there is strong scholarly agreement that the chapter preserves ancient traditions of a covenant-making at Shechem. See, for example: Martin Noth, *Das Buch Josua*, Handbuch zum Alten Testament, VII (Tubingen: J. C. B. Mohr, 1953), p. 139; Jean L'Hour, "L'Alliance de Sichem," *Revue Biblique*, 69 (1962), pp. 34f.; Gerhard von Rad, *The Problem of the Hexateuch and Other Essays*, trans. E. W. Trueman Dicken (Edinburgh: Oliver and Boyd, 1966), pp. 36–40; Hans-Joachim Kraus, *Worship in Israel*, trans. Geoffrey Buswell (Richmond, Va.: John Knox Press, 1966), p. 136; Eduard Nielsen, *Shechem: A Traditio-Historical Investigation* (Copenhagen: G. E. C. Gad, 1959), pp. 85–141.

3. George E. Mendenhall, "The Hebrew Conquest of Palestine," *The Biblical Archaeologist* 25 (1962), pp. 66–100.

4. *Ibid.*, p. 73.

5. Rolf Knierim, "Das Erste Gebot," *Zeitschrift fur die Alttestamentliche Wissenschaft* 77 (1965), pp. 20–39.

6. Albrecht Alt, "Die Wallfahrt von Sichem nach Bethel," *Kleine Schriften zur Geschichte des Volkes Israels.* 3 vols. (Munich: C. H. Beck'sche Verlagbuchhandlung, 1953; 1959), 1:84ff.

7. For a discussion of the tendencies towards monotheism in the ancient world, see: William F. Albright, *From the Stone Age to Christianity* (New York: Anchor Books, 1957), pp. 209–236. The Aton cult of Akhenaton is sometimes considered as genuinely monotheistic. Even so, this does not affect the genuineness of

Israel's worship of Yahweh, for the faith of Akhenaton and his family was never really shared by the Egyptian people; it was by no means a national religion despite the Pharaoh's efforts to make it so.

8. The discovery and interpretation of the Ras Shamra literature has vastly expanded our knowledge of the religious myths, beliefs and practices of the Canaanites. Most of the texts have been published in the journal *Syria* from Vol. 10 (1929) onwards. English translations are found in: Cyrus H. Gordon, *Ugaritic Literature*, Scripta Pontifici Instituti Biblica 98 (Rome, 1949); G. R. Driver, *Canaanite Myths and Legends*, Old Testament Studies 3 (Edinburgh: T. and T. Clark, 1956). A selection is found in James B. Pritchard, ed., *Ancient Near Eastern Texts Relating to the Old Testament*, 3rd ed. (Princeton: Princeton University Press, 1969), pp. 129–155. Periodical literature is extensive.

9. Martin Noth, *Exodus*, trans. J. H. Bowden (London: SCM Press, 1962), p. 190.

10. Kraus, *op. cit.*, p. 72; Martin Noth, *Leviticus*, trans. J. E. Anderson (Philadelphia: The Westminster Press, 1965), p. 186.

11. Anthony Phillips, *Ancient Israel's Criminal Law. A New Approach to the Decalogue* (New York: Schocken Books, 1970), p. 70.

12. Alt, *op. cit.*, 1, pp. 327f.; von Rad, *op. cit.*, p. 85.

13. Cf. Martin Noth, *Numbers*, trans. James D. Martin (Philadelphia: The Westminster Press, 1968), p. 248.

14. Johannes Lindblom, "Lot-casting in the Old Testament," *Vetus Testamentum* 12 (1962), pp. 164–178.

15. Cf. H. Eberhard von Waldow, "Social Responsibility and Social Structure in Early Israel," *Catholic Biblical Quarterly* 32 (1970), p. 192.

16. The Deuteronomic account of the division of the land in Joshua 18:2–12 presents a different picture of the allotment. It takes place after the completion of the well-organized and successful occupation of the land west of the Jordan. Nevertheless, despite its literary-critical complexities and its unhistorical character, it reveals the same two principles of parity and of cultic allotment associated with apportioning of the land in Numbers 26.

17. That it was possible at a later period for a stranger in Israel

to become wealthy is demonstrated by Deuteronomy 28:43f. and Leviticus 25:47ff.

18. Roland de Vaux, *Ancient Israel*, 2 vols., trans. John McHugh (New York: McGraw-Hill Book Company, 1965), 1, p. 83.

II LIBERATION THEOLOGY AND THE CONTEMPORARY SEARCH FOR FREEDOM

Freedom, History, and Hope

JAMES H. CONE

Since the appearance of black theology in North America, liberation theology in Latin America, and political theology in many countries, it is no longer possible to perform Christian theology without taking seriously the question of freedom in history and the hope of humankind. The black struggle for liberation in history, as it is related to oppressed peoples' struggle for liberation throughout the whole world, forces Christian theology to ask: What is freedom and how is it related to oppressed peoples' striving for a humane future?

Freedom is that structure of and movement in human existence which enables people to struggle against slavery and oppression. History is the place in which freedom actualizes itself; and hope is the anticipation of freedom that is actualized in history. Hope is freedom's vision, and history is the context in which the vision takes shape. Freedom, history, and hope are bound together, expressing humanity's constitution, its place and also its future realization. When freedom is separated from history, it is no longer authentic freedom. It is an opium, a sedative which makes people content with freedom's opposite, oppression. Freedom is also denied when it is separated from hope, the vision of a new heaven and a new earth. Hope is freedom's transcendence, the soul's recognition that "what *is* ain't suppose to be." History is freedom's immanence, the recognition that what *is* is the place where we have been called to bear witness to the future, the "not yet" of human existence. Freedom then is a project, not an object. It is the projection of self in history against the structures of oppression in order to bear witness to the coming realm of perfect freedom.

In the light of this perspective on freedom, history and hope, it is possible to reflect on its implications for Scripture, theology and our contemporary situation.

Divine Freedom as the Source of Human Freedom

The human freedom to hope for a new heaven and a new earth is grounded in God's freedom to exist for us in history. This divine freedom must be the Christian starting point of the analysis of freedom, history, and hope. According to Scripture, God's being as freedom not only affirms the divine will to *be* in the divine-self; it is also an affirmation of God's freedom to be *for us* in the social context of human existence. Divine freedom is not merely an affirmation of the existence of God, his complete transcendence over creaturely existence. It also expresses God's will to be in relation to his creatures in the context of their struggle for the fulfillment of humanity. This is the meaning of the Exodus, the Incarnation, and the claim that "Christian theology speaks of God historically." [1] To speak of God historically is to speak of the God who is revealed in history and whose freedom is the divine will to be known in the political context of human strivings for liberation. The biblical God is the God of freedom who calls the helpless and weak into a newly created existence. He is the God of Jesus Christ, the Oppressed One, who came to "put down the mighty from their thrones" and to "exalt those of low degree." He came to "fill the hungry with good things" and to send the rich away empty (Luke 1:52–53). Jesus was born like the poor, was baptized with them, lived among them, and died for them. In Jesus Christ, God disclosed his freedom to take the humiliated condition of the oppressed upon his divine Person so that they might have a new future, different from their past and present miseries. This is why Ernst Käsemann is correct in his contention that "Jesus means freedom." [2] He says, "The Christian faith not only believes in freedom but is already freedom itself. It not only hopes for freedom but, rather, is itself the inauguration of a free life on earth." [3]

When God is revealed in history as freedom for us, the divine is disclosed as a God of hope. "Christian theology," writes Moltmann, "speaks of history eschatologically." [4] To speak of history eschatologically is to speak of the promise of God's Word of liberation, disclosed in his future, breaking into our present and overthrowing the powers of evil that hold people in captivity. The biblical God then is a God of freedom, of history, and of hope.

Divine freedom is the source and content of human freedom. Human freedom, the will to create a new future in history, is grounded in divine freedom, God's will to be for and with us in his future. Because God has created us in freedom and thus wills to be in relation to human beings outside the divine self, freedom is bestowed upon us as a constituent of our created existence. We know, therefore, that we are free not because of the intellectual investigations of idealistic or naturalistic philosophies, but because of a liberating encounter with the One who is the source of freedom. To be content with servitude and oppression is to deny the very ground and intention of our created existence. This is what Anthony Burns, an ex-slave, meant when he said, "God made me a man—not a slave, and gave me the same right to myself that he gave to the man who stole me to himself." [5] A similar point was made by David

Walker when he urged black slaves to remember that freedom is not a gift from white slave masters but a natural right of divine creation:

> Should tyrants take it into their heads to emancipate any of you, remember that your freedom is your natural right. You are men, as well as they, and instead of returning thanks to them for your freedom, return it to the Holy Ghost, who is your rightful owner. If they do not want to part with your labors . . . God almighty, will break their strong band.[6]

Human freedom is not an option that can be given or taken away by oppressors. And people who recognize that essential point can also understand John Cassandra's bold affirmation: "You treated me like a mule and I came out like a man." [7] Human freedom is grounded in God's freedom to be with us in history, disclosing that our future is to be found in the historical struggle against human pain and suffering.

Toward a Definition of Human Freedom

With divine freedom as the point of departure of our theological exploration, we are ready to ask: what is the content of human freedom?

Human freedom is being in relation to God. Since divine freedom is the source and content of human freedom, then it follows that human freedom is freedom for God. Fellowship with God is the beginning and the end of human freedom. The free person is the one who encounters God in faith, that is, in conviction and trust that one's true humanity is actualized only in God.

Human freedom in this sense must now be seen as the very heart of the theological concept of the "image of God," even though this point has too often been obscured. In the history of theology, the image of God has frequently been identified with the human capacity to reason. Theologians since Barth, taking their clue from the Reformation, have of course recognized the relational character of the image of God. But even Barth did not set forth the political and social implications of the divine-human encounter with sufficient clarity. To affirm that human beings are free only when that freedom is derived from divine revelation has concrete political consequences. If we are created for God, then any other allegiance is a denial of freedom, and we must struggle against those who attempt to enslave us. The image of God then is not merely a personal relationship with God, but is also that constitution of humanity which makes all people struggle against captivity. It is the ground of rebellion and revolution among the slaves.

The relational character of freedom as grounded in the human struggle to be free is emphasized in the black spiritual:

> Oh Freedom! Oh Freedom!
> Oh Freedom, I love thee!
> And before I'll be a slave,
> I'll be buried in my grave,
> And go home to my Lord and be free.

Here the theme is freedom in history and struggle against human servitude. Black slaves not only recognized that freedom is essential to human existence ("Oh Freedom! Oh Freedom! Oh Freedom, I love thee!"); but also that freedom is being in relation to God ("And before I'll be a slave, I'll be buried in my grave, and go home to my Lord and be free"). Freedom is not only a relationship with God but an encounter grounded in the historical struggle to be free. "The Christian faith is freedom in struggle, in contradiction, and in temptation." [8]

Freedom Is Being in Relation to Self and the Community of the Oppressed

Freedom is not only being in relation to God; it is being in relation to an oppressed community striving for liberation. To affirm that freedom is the image of God is to say not only who God is but also who I am, and what I am called to be in history. Freedom is knowledge of self; it is a vocation to affirm who I am created to be.

It is clear from divine revelation as witnessed in Scripture that authentic freedom of self is achievable only in the context of an oppressed community struggling for liberation. Because God's freedom for humanity is the divine liberation of the oppressed from bondage, human freedom as response to God's gracious liberation is an act for our brothers and sisters who are oppressed. There can be no freedom for God in isolation from the humiliated and abused. There can be no freedom to be for God unless the hungry are fed, the sick are healed, and justice is given for the poor. "If we believe the crucified Christ to be the representative of God on earth, we see the glory of God no longer in the crowns of the mighty but in the face of the man who was executed on the gallows." [9] To see the freedom of God in the man hanging on a tree means that God's liberation is for those who are falsely condemned and executed in the name of law and order. Black slaves recognized this fact when they focused on the crucified One and saw in Jesus' face their faces, his condition as their condition, his shame as their shame.

> They nail my Jesus down,
> They put him on the crown of thorns,
> O see my Jesus hangin' high!
> He look so pale an' bleed so free:
> O don't you think it was a shame,
> He hung three hours in dreadful pain?

It is most revealing that the slave songs, often called the Black Spirituals, focused more on the Passion and the crucified One than on the nativity of Jesus, although much could have been said about the similarity between the birth of Jesus and that of black slaves. They chose to sing about the One who was "whupped up the hill" and "nailed to the cross." They talked about the One who was "pierced in the side" and how "the blood came twinklin' down." And like black slaves who were rejected, beaten, and shot without a chance to say a word in their defense, Jesus too was humiliated. But he "never said a mumbalin' word/ He jes' hung down his head an' he died." In Jesus' death black slaves saw themselves; they suffered and died with him. James Weldon Johnson expressed the spirit of that reality in poetic and sermonic imagination:

> Jesus, my lamb-like Jesus,
> Shivering as the nails go through his hands;
> Jesus, my lamb-like Jesus,
> Shivering as the nails go through his feet.
> Jesus, my darling Jesus,
> Groaning as the blood came spurting from his wound.
> Oh, look how they done my Jesus.
>
> Oh, I tremble, yes, I tremble,
> It causes me to tremble, tremble,
> When I think how Jesus died;
> Died on the steps of Calvary,
> How Jesus died for sinners,
> Sinners like you and me.[10]

In the slave songs, sermons, and narratives, is revealed God's identity with the poor and the wretched of the earth, affirming the condition of the poor as the condition of the divine. God takes upon his Person black pain and humiliation and discloses that he has come to ease black people's burden and to make their load light. Jesus' resurrection

from the dead is their guarantee that the oppressed have a
future that cannot be destroyed by slave masters and
overseers; so they also sang:

> Weep no more, Martha,
> Weep no more, Mary,
> Jesus rise from the dead,
> Happy Morning.

Persons who do not recognize their freedom as bound up
with the liberation of the poor do not know authentic
freedom. They who define freedom "spiritually," as if the
political freedom of the oppressed is secondary to divine
freedom, do not know Christian freedom and are in fact
alienated from God and in league with the devil.

James Weldon Johnson also wrote:

> We cannot grasp freedom in faith without hearing simulta-
> neously the categorical imperative to serve bodily, social,
> and political obedience for the liberation of the suffering
> creation out of affliction. If we grasp only the promise of
> freedom in faith and forget the realistic demand for the
> liberation of the world, the gospel becomes the religious
> basis for the justification of society as it is and a mystifica-
> tion of the suffering reality.[11]

That human fellowship with God is possible *only* in an
oppressed community is also made clear in the parable of
the Last Judgment in Matthew 25:31f. People are placed
on the right and on the left according to how they minister
to the neighbor. Because the ones on the right met the needs
of the oppressed, they are accepted into the Kingdom, even
though they were not consciously trying to make it there.
For them the neighbor was an end in himself and not a
means to an end. The ones on the left, who are rejected, are
surprised at their rejection because they wanted to make it
in the Kingdom, yet they failed to recognize the connection

between the poor and the Son of man. For if they had
known that the despised were in fact Jesus, they would have
been prepared to help them, because they just wanted to be
in the Kingdom. That is why they said, "Lord, when did we
see thee hungry or thirsty or a stranger or naked or sick or
in prison, and did not minister to thee?" (Matthew 25:44).
The answer was simple: "Truly, I say to you, as you did it
not to one of the least of these, you did it not to me"
(Matthew 25:45).

Freedom is being in history. There is no true freedom
independent of the struggle for liberation in history. History
is the immanent character of freedom; it is freedom's praxis,
the project of freedom. The immanence of freedom is
"visible whenever the emancipation of [people] from the
chains of slavery takes place in history." [12] There is no
freedom without transformation, i.e., without the struggle
for liberation in this world. There is no freedom without the
commitment of a revolutionary praxis against injustice,
slavery, and oppression. Freedom then is not merely a
thought in my head; it is the socio-historical movement of a
people from oppression to liberation—Israelites from Egypt,
black people from American slavery. It is the mind and
body in motion, responding to the passion and the rhythm
of divine revelation, and affirming that no chain shall hold
my humanity down. This is what black slaves meant when
they sang:

> I'm a chile of God wid my soul set free,
> For Christ hab bought my liberty.

A similar point is made in Scripture when divine
revelation is connected with history and salvation is defined
in political terms. In the Old Testament salvation is
grounded in history and is identical with God's righteousness in delivering the oppressed from political bondage. The
Savior is the One who has power to gain victory in battle,

and the saved are the oppressed who have been set free. For Israel Yahweh is the Savior because "the Lord saved [her] that day from the hand of the Egyptians; and Israel saw the Egyptians dead upon the seashore" (Exodus 14:30). That is why the people responded with song:

> I will sing to the Lord, for he has risen up in triumph;
> the horse and his rider he has hurled into the sea.
> The Lord is my refuge and my defense,
> he has shown himself my deliverer. [EXODUS 15:1–2, NEB]

Here salvation is a historical event of rescue. It is God delivering the people from their enemies and bestowing upon Israel new possibilities within the historical context of her existence.

The historical character of freedom is also found in the New Testament. This theme embodies Jesus' life and message and is perhaps best summarized in Luke 7:18ff. When the disciples of John came to Jesus inquiring whether he was the expected messiah, Jesus said, "Go and tell John what you have seen and heard: the blind receive their sight, the lame walk, lepers are cleansed, and the deaf hear, the dead are raised up, the poor have the good news preached to them" (Luke 7:22). Again salvation is not an abstract spiritual idea or a feeling in the heart. Salvation is the granting of physical wholeness in the concreteness of pain and suffering.

Any view of freedom that fails to take seriously a people's liberation in history is not biblical and is thus unrelated to the One who has called us into being. That is why black preachers from Richard Allen to Adam Clayton Powell and Martin Luther King, Jr. viewed slavery and oppression as a contradiction of the divine will. While white missionaries and preachers were saying that "The Freedom which Christianity gives is a Freedom from the Bondage of Sin and Satan, and from the Dominion of Men's Lust and

Passions and inordinate Desires" but "does not make the
least Alteration in Civil property," [13] black preachers were
saying in the spirit of the contemporary black poet, Mari
Evans:

> I take my freedom
> lest I die
> for pride runs through my veins . . .
> For I am he who
> dares to say
> I shall be Free, or dead
> today . . .[14]

Freedom is not a theoretical proposition to be debated in
a philosophy or theology seminar. It is a historical reality,
existing in the struggle for liberation in which an oppressed
people recognize that they were not created to be seized,
bartered, deeded, and auctioned. To understand the *question*
of freedom, we need only hear the words, experience the
mood, and encounter the passion of those who have to deal
with the dialectic of freedom and oppression in the concreteness of their everyday existence.

> Standin' on de corner, weren't doin' no hahm,
> Up come a 'liceman an' he grab me by de ahm.
> Blow a little whistle an' ring a little bell
> Heah come patrol wagon runnin' like hell.
>
> Judge he call me up an' ast mah name.
> Ah tole him fo' sho' Ah weren't to blame.
> He wink at 'liceman, 'liceman wink too;
> Judge say, 'Nigger, you got some work to do?
>
> Workin' on ol' road bank, shackle boun'.
> Long, long time 'fo' six months roll aroun'.
> Miserin' fo' my honey, she miserin' fo' me,
> But, Lawd, white folks won't let go holdin' me.

In this context, freedom is the opposite of the policeman, the judge, and that system which may be loosely described as "white folks," and in the New Testament is called the principalities and powers. Black people do not need a degree in theology or philosophy to know that something is not right about this world. Karl Marx may be helpful in providing a theoretical framework for an articulation of the consciousness of the masses who are victims of economic oppression. But blacks in America and some other places believe that the problem of oppression is much more complex than that. And any analysis that fails to deal with racism, that demon embedded in white folks' being, is *ipso facto* inadequate.

Diggin' in de road bank, diggin' in de ditch,
Chain gang's got me, boss got de switch.
All ah want's dese cold iron shackles off mah leg.

Judge say, "Three Days!" Ah turn aside.
"And ninety nine more years!" Ah hung mah head an' cried.
All ah want's dese cold iron shackles off mah leg.

Of course, freedom is more than the recognition that iron shackles are inhuman; it is also the willingness to do what is necessary to break the chains. As Paulo Freire says, "Nor does the discovery by the oppressed that they exist in dialectical relationship with the oppressor . . . in itself constitute liberation. The oppressed can overcome the contradiction in which they are caught only when this perception enlists them in the struggle to free themselves." [15]

Also it is in the historical context of reflection and action that the oppressed recognize that God is struggling with them in the fight for freedom. This is the meaning of Jesus' lowly birth in Bethlehem, his healing of the sick and demon-possessed, and his death on the cross. God is making plain that his kingdom is not simply a heavenly reality; it is an earthly reality as well. Human beings were not created to work in somebody else's fields, to pick somebody else's cotton, and to live in ghettos among rats and filth. They were created for freedom—for fellowship with God and the projection of self into the future, grounded in historical possibilities. Freedom is self-determination in history and laying claim to that which rightfully belongs to humanity. As Mari Evans puts it:

> I
> am a black woman
> tall as a cypress
> strong
> beyond all definition still
> defying place
> and time
> and circumstance
> assailed
>   impervious
>   indestructible
> Look
>   on me and be
> renewed.[16]

And lest this struggle seem only grim and austere, the same poet sings of its present joy:

> Who
> can be born black
> and not
> sing
> the wonder of it
> the joy
> the challenge
> Who
> can be born
> black
> and not exult! [17]

Freedom is being in hope. While the meaning of freedom includes the historical determination of freedom in this world, freedom is not limited to what is possible in history. There is a transcendent element in the definition of freedom which affirms that the "realm of freedom is always more than the fragments of a free life which we may accomplish in history." [18] I John says it, "Beloved, we are God's children now; it does not appear what we shall be, but we know that when He appears we shall be like Him, for we shall see Him as He is" (3:2). There is included in freedom the "not yet," a vision of a new heaven and a new earth. This simply means that the oppressed have a future not made with human hands but grounded in the liberating promises of God. They have a freedom not bound by human praxis, human strivings to change the social and political structures of existence. In Jesus' death and resurrection, God has freed us to fight against social and political structures while not being determined by them. Black preachers expressed that truth with apocalyptic imagination:

> I know the way gets awful dark sometimes; it looks like everything is against us. Sometimes we wake up in the dark hours of midnight, briny tears flowing down our cheeks, crying and not knowing what we are crying about. But because God is our Captain and is on board now, we can sit still and hear the Word of the Lord. Away back before the wind ever blowed or before the earth was made, Our God had us in mind. He looked down through time one morning and saw you and me and ordained from the very beginning that we should be his children. You remember Old John the Revelator who claimed he saw a number that had come through hard trials and great tribulations and who had washed their robes in the blood of the lamb. Oh, brothers! Ain't you glad that you have already been in the dressing room, because it won't be long before we will take the wings of the morning and go where there will be no more sin and sorrow, no more weeping and mourning.[19]

This sermon makes clear that freedom is also beyond history and not limited to the realities and limitations of this world. God is the sovereign ruler and nothing can prevent his will to liberate the oppressed from being realized.

It is important to note that black theology, while taking history with utmost seriousness, does not limit freedom to history. When people are bound to history, they are enslaved to what the New Testament calls law and death. If death is the ultimate power and life has no future beyond this world, then the rulers of the state who control the policemen and military are indeed our masters. They have our future in their hands and the oppressed can be made to obey laws of injustice. But if the oppressed, while living in history, can nonetheless see beyond it; if they can visualize an eschatological future beyond the history of their humiliation, then "the sigh of the oppressed," to use Marx's phrase, can become a cry of revolution against the established order. It is this revolutionary cry that is granted in the resurrection of Jesus. Freedom then is not simply what oppressed people can accomplish alone; it is basically what God has done and will do to accomplish liberation both in and beyond history. Indeed, because we know that death has been conquered, we are set free to fight for liberation in history—knowing that we have a "home over yonder."

The "home over yonder," vividly and artistically described in the black slave songs, is a gift of divine freedom. If this "otherworldliness" in freedom is not taken with utmost seriousness, then there is no way for the oppressed to be sustained in the struggle against injustice. The oppressed will grow tired and also afraid of the risks of freedom. They will say as the Israelites said to Moses when they found themselves between Pharaoh's army and the sea: "Is it because there are no graves in Egypt that you have taken us away to die in the wilderness? What have you done to us, in bringing us out of Egypt?" (Exodus 14:11). The fear of freedom and the risks contained in the struggle are ever present realities in the fight for liberation. But the tran-

scendence of freedom, granted in Jesus' resurrection, intro-
duces a factor that makes a significant difference. The
difference is not that we are taken out of history while living
on earth—that would be an opiate. Rather it is a difference
that plants our being firmly in history for struggle, because
we know that death is not the goal of history. It was this
truth that enabled black slaves to survive humanely in a
situation of extreme cruelty. To be sure they sang about the
fear of "sinking down" and the dread of being a "motherless
child." They encountered death and the agony of being
alone in an "unfriendly world." But because black slaves
believed that death had been conquered in Jesus' resurrection, they transcended death and interpreted freedom from
death as a heavenly, eschatological reality.

> You needn't mind my dying,
> Jesus' goin' to make up my dying bed.
>
> In my room I know,
> Somebody is going to cry,
> All I ask you to do for me,
> Just close my dying eyes.

Notes

1. Jürgen Moltmann, *Religion, Revolution and the Future*, trans. by
Douglas Meeks (New York: Charles Scribner's Sons, 1969), p.
203.
2. Translated by Frank Clarke (London: SCM Press, 1969).
3. Moltmann, p. 66.
4. *Ibid.,* p. 203.
5. A letter of "Anthony Burns to the Baptist Church at Union,
Fauquier Co., Virginia" in Carter Woodson (ed.), *The Mind of the
Negro as Reflected in Letters Written During the Crisis 1800–1860* (New
York: Russell and Russell, 1969), p. 660.
6. *Walker's Appeal/Garnet's Address* by David Walker and H. H.

Garnet (New York: Arno Press, 1969), pp. 81–82. Walker's *Appeal* was originally published in 1829 and Garnet's address delivered in 1843.

7. Cited in *Long Black Song* by H. A. Baker, Jr. (Charlottesville: University Press of Virginia, 1972), p. 116.

8. Moltmann, p. 66.

9. *Ibid.,* p. 68.

10. James Weldon Johnson, *God's Trombones* (New York: Viking Press, 1972), pp. 42, 43.

11. *Ibid.,* p. 95.

12. *Ibid.,* p. 79.

13. Cited in H. Richard Niebuhr, *The Social Sources of Denominationalism* (Cleveland: Meridian Books, 1929), p. 249.

14. *I Am A Black Woman* (New York: William Morrow and Company, 1970), p. 75.

15. *Pedagogy of the Oppressed*, trans. by M. A. Ramos (New York: Herder and Herder, 1970), p. 34.

16. Mari Evans, *I Am A Black Woman*, p. 12.

17. *Ibid.,* p. 93.

18. Moltmann, p. 79.

19. Langston Hughes and Arna Bontemps (eds.), *Book of Negro Folklore* (New York: Dodd, Mead & Co., 1958), pp. 252–253. (Paraphrased).

Grace: Power for Transformation

T. RICHARD SHAULL

Over the past 20 years I have lived in Latin America and had a great deal of contact with Latin American theologians of liberation. But in this essay, I have decided not to write primarily about them or their situation. If I have learned anything in recent years, it is that authentic theological reflection cannot be imported. If we want to think theologically about liberation, then it is *our own liberation* that must concern us. If along that road we meet Latin Americans engaged in the same struggle, a dialogue with them may be important to all concerned. But given our tendency to borrow our theologies from other parts of the world and other people's experiences, I prefer now to consider *my* struggle for liberation and the possibilities I see for reflection upon it; I trust that in approaching the problem this way, others will be encouraged to follow a similar route.

I am a white, middle class, male, North American. By each of these adjectives I identify and confess my involvement in the construction of prisons for the great mass of human beings living in the world today. Prisons in which humanity is violated, basic material needs are unmet, and cherished expectations unfulfilled. Prisons in which men and women are transformed into objects, denied the excitement of living that can come only as they dance to their own rhythm and shape their own destiny. I am also a

Christian, and I recognize that my life has been and is very much shaped by that fact. I am a Christian who tries to think—about my faith and its relation to what is going on in the world and in my life today, about the power it offers for living and how it can be appropriated. Because I am a Christian I have felt compelled over the years to try to atone for my guilt as someone who is white, bourgeois, male, and North American. In Latin America, I chose to identify myself with those who considered me the enemy and be part of their revolution. It worked for a while but in the end we all suspected there was something phony about it. Then I returned to the States to join in the struggle of those who shared my belief that our system here was demonic and should be confronted and attacked head-on. And with many of them, I also discovered that this confrontation did not threaten to destroy the system but did threaten to destroy us. However radical we were, we did not really get at the roots of the dehumanizing forces of our society. Now, older and I hope a bit wiser because of these years of experience, I find myself compelled to start over again at a different point. I, a constructor of prisons for most of the rest of the world, am myself a prisoner. In fact, I have helped actively to build the walls which imprison me; I have allowed others to build those prison walls around me without any strenuous objections on my part.

I suspect that most of you are also prisoners, and that you have had your part in building your own walls. I cannot identify the blocks that make up the walls that close you in. I can only point to a few which do that to me.

I am the prisoner of an absurd economic order, based on the continuous expansion of production of consumer goods for that small portion of the world's population that can afford them. I know this economic system ignores the most basic needs of the world's population when it could be used to meet those needs. I also know that this type of economic growth, in the course of the next hundred years, will probably exhaust our natural resources, pollute our environment to the point where human life may be impossible, and force us to police the world to maintain our affluence while millions will be literally starving to death.

I am the prisoner of a "democratic" political system which leaves me completely powerless, a system largely controlled by the incestuous relationship now existing between large corporations and the government, a form of bureaucratic organization unable to deal with the decay of our cities, the need for housing for our population, the energy crisis, and a host of other problems becoming more acute every day.

I am also the prisoner of institutions that once structured life-giving relationships but which now tend to limit life, growth and creativity. This is true in our educational system from the primary school to the university. It is evident in the structure of marriage and family life.

Finally, I have allowed myself to be convinced that my prison is not really a prison. It's reality; that's just the way it is. If I begin to suspect that all this is a myth and that I have been brainwashed, those who run the prison have an extraordinary capacity to make me doubt my intuition and get me to conform. My timid desire to do something to improve the situation is encouraged and sometimes praised, but I suspect that what I am really doing is merely cementing the cracks of the prison walls.

Worst of all, I discover a disintegrating social order that threatens to take me down with it, and has left me and many of the young people I know today with no resources to break away or to change it, with no compelling vision of a new and more human social order, with no clear options for doing anything about change. A competitive society incapable of nourishing community life has left us psychically deprived; most of the limited energy we have is drained off in trying to hold ourselves together and create some little space in which to live.

If this is my situation, what are my chances for liberation? And how can I achieve it? Certainly not by concen-
trating my attention on social and political group actions of
a liberal or radical sort. To stick with the prison analogy a
little longer, my prison is filled with the bodies of those who,
during the last few years, have been shot down attempting
this and with many more who simply collapsed before they
had really begun to fight.

If I am to have any hope of eventually breaking out of
my prison and participating in the creation of a more
human *polis,* then I have no choice but to get to the very
sources of my life and energy and discover how to renew
them; to radically change my system of values; to develop a
new sense of who I am and what I want—a new subjectivity
and intentionality. And since I cannot do that by myself, I
must find a few people here and there who can give life to
each other day in and day out.

Thirty years ago, Eugen Rosenstock-Huessy, a German
social philosopher and historian, expressed what he perceived to be the human situation:

> The modern individual—externally a homeless, shiftless,
> noncommittal nomad, internally a jig-saw puzzle of nervous
> conflicts—is the very opposite of the Christian patriarchs to
> whom after 1500 the gospel was addressed. He is far too
> weak to stand alone. He cannot justify himself by faith, for
> he is a natural unbeliever—not simply in religious matters,
> but in relation to himself and the basic instincts and
> decisions of ordinary life. To try to convert him in the
> traditional manner and ask him to begin with a confession
> of sin would be a hopeless proceeding. Not until we take the
> burden of loneliness from him, and restore his natural
> powers of belief through a new experience of living with his
> fellowmen in shared hope, can we expect a rebirth of
> Christian faith in him.
>
> [*The Christian Future,* pp. 40–41]

You may say: that's all very well! But if we hope to break

down prison walls and create new institutional forms of human relationships, that requires power; it is a matter of political strategy and struggle. What I am trying to focus on is the question, "What shape does politics take today if we take seriously both the social situation we are in and what it has done to us as persons?" I can offer the following responses:

I can fight like hell to keep from being used to repair the walls that enclose me but are slowly crumbling around me. I don't have to allow myself to be co-opted to support programs of liberal reform or burn up my energies in such activities. To have worked for the impeachment of President Nixon, supported legislation to control campaign spending, given large amounts of time to committees and have developed a new curriculum for the seminary where I teach; these are things I spend my time on without any expectation that I am doing something significant to change the present order. I might get involved in one or another of them for quite different reasons.

I can look at the prison walls around me with something of an apocalyptic sense. However powerful they may seem, their foundations are cracking. At one point or another they may collapse when we least expect it. The energy crisis has only begun to shake the foundations of our economic order and of our way of life. So far no one has really dealt with the basic issues it raises. We can't expect that to happen until the problem becomes much more acute and renders most of our solutions obsolete before they ever get approved, much less implemented. The decay of our major cities, the housing crisis, the incapacity of an affluent society to meet the needs of vast numbers of its members: these, in my judgment, are only a few signs of the coming apocalypse.

To expect the apocalypse does not mean to sit back and do nothing. It does mean to refuse to buy into the American myth, to sit tight with our present structures and institutions, to discard obsolete categories and search for new ones, to develop a new social vision and propose radically different solutions to our major problems. The apocalypse is not the end; it is the beginning. When the old order crumbles, we will be threatened with chaos and anarchy. But that is also a moment to be seized by creative spirits who can offer a way ahead and act decisively.

We cannot, by some old or new political strategy, bring down the walls of our prison. We also cannot escape from it. But we can join with a few kindred spirits to create a small liberated zone in which all sorts of interesting things can happen. It can be a space where the spell of the dominant system is broken; where men and women discover they can be alive in the midst of the deadness around them; where our perception of what's wrong with society is sharpened by constant critical examination of what is happening to us and to those confined by diverse social structures.

In such a liberated zone we can gradually develop human relationships which increase awareness and stimulate growth; relationships that provide support and solidarity in the midst of chaos and conflict with the established order. We can experiment with processes of ongoing transformation—both personal and social. And we can think about social, economic and political problems in new ways and test out alternatives to what we now have. For what is called for today, in one area after another is re-invention, and a liberated zone may offer us the context in which to experiment. To live in such a milieu and bring the resources of that experience into the major areas of struggle for the transformation of our common life—that, in my judgment, is of the essence of the struggle for liberation in our society at this time.

But the task of creating a liberated zone within the confines of our prison borders on the absurd, since our imprisonment has broken our wills and left us without hope. Indeed, the task we have defined does border on the absurd—unless we can be transported from the realm of the imperative into the sphere of grace where new life is offered to us as a gift, when we least expect it. For me, when we reach this point, the political question becomes a religious question closely connected to the core of the Christian heritage. To experience life, the struggle for transformation of ourselves and of our society, as grace is an affirmation of faith with striking significance for our time. Although the word grace may no longer communicate much to us, it points toward a particular way of experiencing life and the world: toward the discovery that, when we mourn the loss of what we most cherish, we are often surprised by an experience of life that goes beyond anything we have known before; toward the possibility, time and again, of ordering our world in meaningful ways in the midst of personal and social disintegration; toward an awareness that when we are trapped in a closed situation, we can at times break out of it and start over again—and discover new options we did not know existed; toward the gradual recovery of hope as we live a new history, a history of venturing forth in these and other situations, expecting to be surprised and grasped by a power not our own.

Dare I affirm all this in face of the reality around us? When I am surrounded by so many broken men and women who apparently have no reason for living and nowhere to go? When I see what happens so often to those creative spirits who try to defy the deathly structures around them? When I cannot escape the fact that millions of people around the world are suffering and dying, and that there seems to be no way of avoiding it?

Yes, I stick with my affirmation even though I have no adequate answer to the questions that are posed again and again. I stick with it because all the rational responses leave no room for the objective reality—which is at the same time a mystery—by which I am apprehended: my own experience of grace, my participation in a loosely structured but nonetheless real community of men and women who share and are sustained by that same experience, ambiguous and yet at times powerful witness of a community of faith to that same reality.

Over many centuries this experience of grace was mediated by powerful symbols, by a rich language connected with our daily experience of life, by liturgy and sacrament, and by the church as a community living out grace in human relationships. For many of the young people I know these elements have little if any power. Even for myself and others of my generation, those things which once functioned in a powerful way are more of a memory than a present reality.

Today, grace is apprehended through men and women who experience it, make it visible in their lives and in their relationships with others. Consequently, as a theologian I am not primarily interested in developing a new theological language to speak about grace nor in translating the traditional terms into contemporary idiom. What I am concerned with is the incarnation of grace in our situation, and the ongoing effort to give form and visibility to the operation of grace in the midst of the human struggle for liberation.

This is a multi-faceted task. It is a matter of experience and the interpretation of that experience. It may lead us to explore the vision and power of new and (for us) strange forms of spirituality and religious experience. It will, I believe, force us into more serious dialogue with therapists and others engaged in the ministry of healing.

These are long term projects and I have very little to say about them at this time. I do want to focus your attention on something else: my conviction that the experience of grace in the midst of the struggle for liberation has certain important and specific elements in it. In other words, a large part of our problem is knowing what to look for and where to look for it. And on that score, I find myself drawing more and more on certain lines of the Christian tradition which can clarify and empower my thought and action.

There is a persistent strain in Christian thought and experience that breaks through from time to time. Some of the early Church Fathers expressed it this way: God became man so man might become divine. When that tradition is at work, a strange drive is injected into history: women and men expect to become more than they are; their own lives and their relationships with others are full and meaningful as they keep moving beyond themselves.

From time to time I meet people who exemplify this. When I do, I recognize a beautiful and powerful thing, and I rejoice in it. I see men and women under sentence of death who refuse to die, who in the midst of a dying culture are turned on to life; men and women who are unwilling to accept the limits set for them, or to function according to the terms established by the culture and institutions of which they are a part; men and women who cannot tolerate the limited alternatives offered to them and who dare to imagine and give form to other options that previously did not exist; men and women who are willing to live without answers and accept each tentative experience as the occasion to initiate a new process of questioning; men and women who have developed special antennae for detecting where our system is not working, for getting hold of and bringing to consciousness the contradictions in our society and its institutions; and perhaps most important, women and men who discover that as they live this way, they give life to each other and know the joy and pain of relationships that are ever growing.

In recent years I have been fascinated by Saint Paul's understanding of the world as an ongoing process of death and resurrection. I experience grace most powerfully in the midst of that process, and I am convinced that it offers a perspective of special relevance to our present situation. Within that perspective, we are free to bury our dead when their time has come. In periods of social disintegration, nothing accelerates that process more than our desperate attempt to hold on to what is most problematic. To open the way to the future in a time of crisis we must admit that certain relationships, institutions and structures have outlived their time. It is only as we bury them that we clear the way for the re-structuring of our common life.

We can also learn how to accept and live through a real death experience as we critically examine the values we most cherish. We can let go of ideas, goals, and ways of living and working that no longer serve us. We can look for rather than hide from the anomalies of experience. When we do this, we will certainly face chaos, anxiety and insecurity; we may also be surprised by a new life we could never have experienced without passing through that death.

To go one step further, we can bring death into the midst of life and break its power. When we accept in our daily consciousness the precariousness of all that is most precious to us, then we are really free to live most intensely in the present and allow a richer tomorrow to unfold.

A number of anthropologists tell us that when people experience a profound cultural breakdown, their whole way of putting and holding their world together falls apart. When that happens, they move ahead only as they give up the myths and values they previously held to, and discover a new way of putting their world together again. In theological terms, this is the emergence of a new redemptive process. And it is precisely this that religious movements of revitalization have offered to human communities in crisis.

Finally, the incarnation of grace today means the creation of a new individual and group identity over and against the dominant system, and the development of life styles and relationships which point toward a more human life in a technological society. This calls for an attitude of disloyalty toward our present values and institutions out of loyalty to a dim but emerging vision of a more human future. It entails a culture of deviance from the established structures of death in which we are caught.

Many blacks in our society have arrived at this point. A growing number of women are moving in the same direction. I hope that this process will not be so limited in the future, but that it will expand to include a wider and growing circle of men and women. I also trust that it will eventually produce strong centers of life and of creativity and an atmosphere in which freedom, imagination and life-giving human relationships will have a chance to survive and infiltrate the communities and institutions of which they are a part.

Most of us, whatever our political position, are not prepared to undertake this task. We have a very limited sense of what it takes to sustain such a radical stance. But I wager that the formation of such communities is possible; that it is going to happen in the next few years, and that within these communities we will be grasped by a new experience of grace.

Here again we as Christians have at our disposal the resources of a rich history. Several years ago I took part in a series of discussions with Herbert Marcuse at Temple University. To my surprise this Marxist philosopher was interested in discussing sectarian religious movements, not Marxism, because he was looking increasingly to them for insights and power with which to respond to the challenge posed by our advanced technological society. Perhaps sooner or later others will get around to the same thing.

At this point you may well want to ask if what I have just said is a theological statement. My answer is categorically in the affirmative. It is the only way of speaking of theology today that makes any sense to me. For what can be more theological than an attempt to describe the meaning and power of grace in the struggle for personal and social transformation in which we are now engaged? To be sure, I have not developed a systematic theological argument in traditional terms. I believe that theology will speak more directly to the human condition if it remains incognito, at least for the time being.

I am also convinced that we have a lot of homework ahead of us. We need to be much more in touch with our own religious history and with a wider community of faith —in touch with it and engaged in the task of re-working it. It is important to search for new patterns of reflection and new forms of rationality which will deal more authentically and adequately with the subject matter of theology. The historians and exegetes among us can provide tools for a new dialogue with our past. I cannot predict how far all this can go, how long it will take, or what it will produce. But I take on my share of this task expectantly, for I believe that out of it will emerge a new language and new symbols with power for creative living in this time.

Liberation Theology in a Feminist Perspective

LETTY M. RUSSELL

These are especially exciting and challenging times for women.
Exciting, because so many new ideas, life styles and ways of
service are opening up. Challenging, because they are often
moving away from old securities to new paths where there
are many questions and few answers. Every field of
learning, every skill, every life style becomes a new arena of
experiment as women seek out their own perspectives and
the contribution that they can make in building a new
house of freedom.

Theology is no exception to this excitement and challenge. Women are voicing their search for liberation by
rejecting oppressive and sexist religious traditions that
declare them to be socially, ecclesiastically and personally
inferior. They are digging deeper into their traditions,
raising questions about the authority of the church "fathers," and searching out the hidden contributions of the
church "mothers" to the life and mission of the church.
They are looking for truly authentic and liberating roots as
they search for a usable past. At the same time, women are
joining other oppressed groups in seeking out a clear vision
of a new society of justice and *shalom*, so that they can join
the global struggle for a usable future.[1]

These women advocate changes that will establish political, economic and social equality of the sexes. In a Christian context they reflect on how theology can become more complete, as all people are encouraged to contribute to the meaning of faith from their own perspective. Such action and theory forms the basis of feminist theology. It is feminist because those involved are actively engaged in advocating the equality and partnership of women and men in church and society.

Feminist theology has common roots with many types of so-called Third World liberation theologies. With male domination of the social structures, women have a growing consciousness of their own oppression. Some women have adopted the term Fourth World, referring to themselves as an oppressed world majority. Barbara Burris writes, "We identify with all women of all races, classes, and countries all over the world. The female culture is the Fourth World." [2]

Like Third World liberation theology, feminist theology arises from an experience of oppression in society. It interprets the search for salvation as a journey toward freedom; as a process of self-liberation in community with others. Together with other people searching for freedom, women speak of hope. They want to tell the world that they are part of God's plan of *human* liberation.

It is my strong conviction that feminist theology and Third World liberation theologies have much to gain from each other. In their initial phases, both movements considered concrete forms of oppression. Time was also devoted to the legitimization of their particular theology against white, Western, male theology. These things continue to be important, but they should not prevent us from acknowledging the common ground between liberation theologies and the possibilities of cooperation in both action and reflection. Often oppressed groups have been so busy in asserting the importance of their own perspectives and agendas that they have exercised horizontal violence against each other. They have played the oppressor's game, vying for top place on the list of the "Hit Parade of Oppressions." Recognizing that racism is the most serious cancer in American society, we must, nevertheless, remember that sexism and classism are intertwined with racist oppression and that all these appear in world-wide manifestations of cruelty which might make our own present positions seem enviable.

This essay will raise some of the important issues in liberation theology that are already on our common agenda and present some notes on common methodologies and perspectives which appear in the action and reflection of various liberation theologies. It will then examine some of the insights of feminist theology in relation to style and method as well as some of the problems of the feminist perspective, and conclude with a brief discussion of liberation theology and the problem of tradition.

Liberation Theology

Feminists and Third World groups share a common ground in what is coming to be called liberation theology, since both are concerned with the gospel message of liberation interpreted as good news for the oppressed. There are many types of liberation theology and no one narrow school dominates because this type of reflection grew out of many struggles to interpret the meaning of the gospel in the light of concrete actions for social change.

For the purpose of stressing common methodologies and perspectives we shall say liberation theology consists of reflection upon the experience of oppression and divine-human action toward the creation of a more humane society. This form of political theology or the theology of hope is expressed by such writers as Jürgen Moltmann, Johannes Metz and Dorothee Sölle.[3] According to Molt-

mann, Christian political theology attempts to relate the
eschatological message of freedom to socio-political reality.
The focus of Christian hope is not simply on the future, but
on the future of the hopeless.

Common methodologies. In general, liberation theologians
stress an inductive rather than a deductive approach.
Instead of deducing conclusions from first principles of
Christian tradition and philosophy, many people today
approach theology reflecting on their life experience as it
relates to the gospel message, stressing the situation-variable
nature of the gospel only when it speaks concretely to their
particular need for liberation.

For this reason liberation theologians address experiences
that illuminate their own situation and can be shared with
others. They try to express the gospel in the light of the
oppression out of which the gospels were written, whether
racial or sexual, social or economic, psychological or
physical. Such a method draws upon many disciplines that
illuminate the human condition, not just on a particular
theological tradition.

This inductive approach is experimental in nature. It is a
theology of constantly revised questions and tentative
insights about a changing world, rather than the type of
theology described by Thomas Aquinas as a "science of
conclusions." [4] In developing new models for thinking about
God in a Christian context, women pose a vast array of
questions addressed to biblical and church tradition and to
the concepts of creation, redemption, sin, salvation and
incarnation. No doctrine is left unchallenged in the search
for a faith that can shape life amidst rapid and sometimes
chaotic change. "These doctrines are no longer taken so
much as answers than as ways of formulating questions." [5]

Such an approach is heavily dependent on the corporate
support of the community out of which it grows. Just as
black theology grows out of the American black community
and black churches, feminist theology grows out of small

communities of women experimenting together in actions and reflection.

This communal search is doubly important because liberation theology is intended to be practiced. It is a tool for change used by those who believe in the biblical promises for the oppressed. Liberation thinking flows not only "downward" from the "theological experts" but also upward from the collective experience of action and ministry. It is practical theology that brings action and reflection together. Thus liberation theology is not usually systematic, and does not place all its discoveries or conclusions into one over-arching system. Instead it concentrates on applying discoveries to bring about change.

Common perspectives. Liberation theologies share at least three common perspectives. The first is that the biblical promise of liberation is an important part of theological reflection.[6] Two major motifs of the Bible are liberation and universality. God is portrayed in both the Old and New Testaments as the liberator, not just of one small nation or group, but of all humankind. This theme is an important part of the biblical understanding of God's *oikonomia* or action for the world in the history of salvation. God's *oikonomia* provides an eschatological perspective. Because we see ourselves as part of "God's utopia," we participate as Christians in the work of liberation. As Paul says in I Corinthians 9:17, "we are entrusted with a commission *(oikonomian)*." Participation is the way we express hope and confidence in God's intention of liberation and salvation. No longer are lines drawn between Christian and non-Christian, or between one confession and another. Instead, Christians join with all those involved in the revolution of freedom, justice and peace.

This theology stresses the gospel's good news of liberation. Christ has set the captives free and, therefore, there is hope for the future. This hope stems, not just from our own actions and strategies, that are often weak and misguided, but from God's promise for all humanity. In the women's movement many reject the Bible as the basis for theology because of the patriarchal, cultural attitudes it reveals. Yet those who would embrace Christian theology cannot abandon the story of Jesus of Nazareth. Instead they must use the best tools of scholarship, wrestle with the texts, and find out how liberation and universality apply to their own experience.

A second perspective shared by most liberation theologies is that individual and world history are both changing and changeable.[7] The Bible views the world as a series of meaningful events that are moving toward the fulfillment of God's plan and purpose for salvation. Each human being is made up of his or her individual history, and society is formed out of collective events and histories. This historical process takes on meaning as we interpret the events that shape our future. The future is at the disposal of those who are aware of their own historical possibility and seek out political, economic and social ways of planning for tomorrow. For Christians there is also a vision of a future that comes when God places it at our disposal.[8] Through hope in God's future we find new courage and strength to enter into the difficult process of planning and acting on behalf of human liberation. We enter the struggle against oppression because we are driven by the knowledge that the "gospel's business is the liberation of human beings. . . . Having faith, we put our wager on the liberation of all people." [9] We also enter the struggle because to be human is to take part in this historical process of transforming the world and shaping the future.[10]

To look at world history requires us to become involved in the development of ideologies or sets of ideas that change and shape reality. Christians, along with others, make use of these in order to participate in the revolutions of freedom. Christian women make use of the ideology of women's liberation, some Christian blacks relate to the ideology of black power, and some Latin Americans ally themselves with Marxist ideology.

The difficulty of this dangerous but important mix of faith and ideology is that ideologies are only partial interpretations of social reality. For Christians all ideologies must be subject to a constant critique in the light of the gospel, yet neither God nor ideologies provide us with a blueprint of the future. God's promise leads us to a confidence that the future is open, but not to an exact knowledge of how liberation will be accomplished or what it will look like. With faith, we must live with the poverty of that knowledge.

A third common perspective of most liberation theologies is that of salvation as a social event. In Christian theology today there is a new awareness of social relationships. This has led to a broader understanding of individual salvation to include the beginnings of salvation in the lives of all who identify with Jesus, the Liberator.[11] Often the Old Testament concept of salvation as *shalom* is stressed, a peace based upon wholeness and total social well-being in community with others.

Emphasis is placed on the longed-for eternal life as a quality of existence in the here and now. It is expressed through actions as we try to share God's gift of liberation with all people. Thus, salvation is not an escape from fate or nature; it is a transformation of the world, bringing a new creation, and seeking to overcome suffering.

In this perspective sin is the opposite of liberation, sin is oppression; it is that situation in which there is no community, no room to live as a whole human being.[12] Sin "is eminently a political, a social term."[13] It includes the sins of our own people, race and class. Therefore, we are faced with responsibility not only for admitting our collaboration but also for working to change the social structures that bring it about.

Obviously, not all people engaged in liberation theology

would choose to underline these particular common methodologies or perspectives. Certainly there are many other themes and emphases that could be lifted up along with these. Yet, insofar as various liberation theologies are engaged in a common enterprise, this provides some ground for fruitful exploration by liberation theologians as they seek out the meaning of Jesus Christ in the midst of a world groaning for freedom (Rom. 8:18–25).

Feminist Theology

There are, of course, many types of feminist theologies, but for the purpose of this essay I will describe feminist theology as reflection on the meaning of God's will to bring about full human liberation and the partnership of women and men in church and society. This theology is called *feminist* because it is professed by those who advocate the equality of the sexes. Yet such theology is not necessarily limited to the female.

Feminist theology arises from the experience of oppression of women in an androcentric society that considers women to be "not-quite human."[14] A society that sets up white males as the standards of humanity inevitably reinforces certain cultural myths that are internalized by the oppressed groups. The result is the formation of racist and sexist castes in the society. Feminist theology is a search for liberation from oppression by those who advocate human personhood for all. As such, it can be advocated by both males and females and it can emphasize a variety of feminine and masculine traits. Its distinctive message concerns not the female or the feminine, but the *feminist* advocacy of full personhood for women as well as men. There are only a few books specifically in this area of theology, although the number of articles is increasing and several books are being published this year.[15]

Insights. Over the past few years feminist theology has

developed insights which can be shared with other liberation theologies. Many of these relate to the basic content of
Christian tradition. Here I would only like to suggest some
of the insights that relate to the feminist style or method of
doing theology.

One such insight is the emphasis on sisterhood leading to
collective efforts in theology.[16] Much written theology has
come out of extensive group discussion. It is not "handed
down from the top," but emerges from group consciousness
and struggle.[17] Women have gone this route partly out of
necessity. It was necessary to overcome violence among
women in order for women to support one another. This
called for intentional cooperative efforts. Also the disinterest
of male theologians and the lack of other female theologians
as role models caused women to band together and carry
out their research in an experimental manner.

Other insights grew from corporate style. For instance,
women discovered that they need not be rigorously linear or
systematic in style. As they began to speak out of their own
life stories, women discovered that their wholistic view of
life, inclusive of emotions and the totality of experience
along with the mind, could be brought to play in the
theological enterprise. For this reason many women gain in
reflection through drama, celebration, music and story and
not just through argumentation.[18]

Consciousness raising has led to the development of new
stories of faith, and in turn has led to new research and
interpretation of the biblical story and Christian history, as
well as to a new language that is clearly inclusive of women
in the Christian tradition.[19] Women are seeking pronouns
that indicate that *both* women and men are included in the
words expressed. The English usage of such words as *man,
men, his, mankind, brotherhood,* etc., in the generic sense has
been increasingly called into question. However much a
particular person or organization may protest that the

words really mean human, human beings, his and hers, humankind, personhood, etc., the fact remains that women are frequently left out of both the mental and social structures of our culture. This struggle with language extends to the reconsideration of the words and images for the Trinity as well as other issues.[20]

Problems. Like other liberation theologies, feminist theology has a tendency to be what is sometimes called genitive theology: a theology *of* women. Writers sometimes think that it is not only *by* women, but also *about* women. Yet, feminist theology is not necessarily by women or about women. It is about God. When women do it, they speak of feminist theology in order to express their own experience out of which they perceive and join in God's actions. Another way of expressing this is to say that the life situation of their theology is that of women living in a particular time and place.

Women's theological reflections are as important as that of any group around the world. They make a contribution to the unfinished dimension of Christian thought. Women want to add to the understanding of the Christian faith, not to replace the other insights that have been contributed by others, and as they add their small piece of experience about the way God is known to them to all the other pieces, the totality of Christian thinking becomes more wholistic and comprehensive.

The problem with their contributions, however, is that they are sometimes so overwhelmed with their new consciousness of selfhood or with bitterness toward the injustices of the church, that they focus only on the narrow self-story of women. This frequently happens when there is such a strong identification with the women's liberation ideology that the center of the Christian message in Jesus Christ is lost.[21] The problem of Christian tradition surfaces as women struggle to distinguish between culturally oppressive patriarchal traditions in the Bible and church history, and the core of tradition itself as reflected in God's will to hand over Jesus Christ to all generations and groupings of people.

Two key problems in feminist theology related to this narrowing of focus to genitive theology, are racism and classism. The women writing most of this literature are mainly educated, white, Western women. In order to speak to black and other Third World women, they need to be inclusive of the particular experiences of oppression of these groups. Only as the women's movement begins to include more and more of these women and to reflect their concerns will it truly be a "Fourth World movement" of women in every race, class and country.[22] Feminist theology must speak to the various situations of women's oppression and interpret these clearly in the light of the gospel message if it is to avoid a narrow parochialism of one class and culture of women.[23] The danger is always present that it too will "cop-out" from addressing itself to the interlocking system of racism, classism and sexism operative in society.[24] It needs to assist in the prophetic task of criticizing the women's movement when the movement is geared to maintaining privileges for white, middle class women at the expense of the vast remainder of the economically and racially oppressed peoples of the world.

One of the key issues to be examined in addressing all of these problems is the meaning of Christian tradition and the way women relate to the message of the Christian gospel and help that message to come alive in their lives. It is to this discussion of tradition that we now turn in order to clarify the meaning of theological rootedness in feminist and other liberation theologies.

Liberation Theology and the Problem of Tradition

Human beings need to find identity and strength from images of the past which can help to guide them in shaping their present and future. Such a past that is still living, evolving, and meaningful is not always easy to find. Some persons and groups are ignorant or ashamed of their past. Others have a history which is full of sorrow and pain. But, whatever the past may be, it becomes usable through reflection on its meaning. Research into the hidden past of oppressed people frees them to gain a sense of history on which to build their future. Combined with a contemporary history of actions to change their world, such a usable past helps in the search for a usable future.[25]

Liberation theology can help in the search for a usable past because it reflects on the love of God in Jesus Christ and establishes this as the basis of the future. It can aid us in seeking out the tradition of Christ in our lives, not only from the past events of His life, death and resurrection, but also from the present and future events of His liberating power. Because we remember the past and live with it as the promise of the future, we remember the future God has promised us. It is this memory which makes us "prisoners of hope" (Zech. 9:12).

One of the problems faced by all liberation theologies is how to deal creatively and faithfully with tradition. How do we seek out the usable past which strengthens participation in shaping a usable future? Often our work does not deal sufficiently with the importance of reflecting, not only on our actions, but also on the tradition which provides perspective on God's future. Thus, if we are to continue to pursue the methodology associated with liberation theology, it is necessary to examine the problem of tradition.

A usable past and future. Recent currents in the ecumenical discussion of tradition are marked by the discovery that tradition is a problem in the light of historicity. Since World War II scholars have tried to understand the relation of the "revolutionary world" to tradition and to pre-war history. In Protestant circles there has been a rediscovery of tradition as an important element in theology, and in

Roman Catholic circles theologians have begun to realize that an explicit theology of tradition is a recent nineteenth century development.

Both Protestant and Roman Catholic scholars have been attempting to find a common understanding of tradition as expressed in both written and unwritten forms. Recognizing that both scripture and tradition are forms of the gospel of Jesus Christ, scholars have begun to emphasize distinctions within the meaning of the word tradition. In historical and theological investigations, distinctions are being made between *Tradition* (the handing over of Jesus Christ; cf. Matthew 12:22; Romans 8:31–32), and *traditions* (particular confessional patterns).

Tradition is now being recognized as a basic anthropological category related to change as the medium of human existence. The writings of such theologians as Gerhard Ebeling clearly reflect a shift from the primary system of static ontological categories of thought to the secondary system of changing, historical categories of thought and action.[26] This approach turns from the attitude of the Middle Ages toward tradition as a repository of the past, to that of the modern world which understands tradition as meaningful events committed to shaping the present and the future.

Tradition which constantly makes use of past experience and events in order to shape the present and future, is an important tool for liberation theology. It gives those who are oppressed or seeking to change the status quo a means for sifting out history and rejecting those elements that form the ideologies and myths behind oppression. For liberation theology, which views the world and humanity as historical and changing, tradition encompasses a process of conscientization or coming to awareness of one's self and world in order to transform it. This process can provide a means of shaping a more humane tradition which points toward a usable future for all humanity.

Tradition as Mission. When we take a new look at tradition we see that Tradition (in its particular sense of handing over Jesus Christ) and God's mission belong to the same theological spectrum. Both are dependent on the action of God in Christ; both have a living, active quality which calls for decision concerning present and future. Both find their clarification not in polemics, but in differentiation between understanding of God's action, and the derivative understanding of the various activities of women and men. The nature of *missio Dei* is understood in biblical perspective as the sending action and *oikonomia* of God in the history of the world. The church participates in this mission by its missionary or sending activity in the world. Tradition is another way of describing this sending activity of God in which men and women participate through the shaping of traditions and of history.[27]

According to biblical investigations, the basis of *paradosis* (tradition) in the New Testament is God's action in Jesus Christ (Romans 8:31–32). Karl Barth has suggested that before anything happened in the life story of Jesus, God handed him over to men and women. This action of God is the "aboriginal *traditum*" that "stands at the center of the New Testament, as the chief topic of both the apostolic kerygmata and doxologies." [28] The deliverance of Jesus is part of God's eternal plan to redeem humanity. "The Son of Man is to be delivered *(paradidosthai)* into the hands of men" and women (Matthew 17:22). The origin of all deliverance is found in God's *paradosis* by which the Son becomes "the first object and bearer of all salvific tradition. . . ." [29] Christ continues the process through the witness of the apostles and the inspiration of the Holy Spirit.[30] This Spirit, which is "poured out," inaugurating the messianic age, inspires the tradition in human hearts so that it continues to be living, dynamic and missionary.

In the light of some recent currents in the discussion of tradition and mission it is possible to say that tradition is

mission because its very description is that of God's
missionary activity in handing Christ over into the hands of
women and men in order that all people may come to the
truth (I Timothy 2:4). The tradition is thus God's handing
over of Jesus Christ into the hands of all generations and
nations until Christ hands all things back to God. The
action of tradition is God's missionary activity in sending
Christ. The object of the activity is Christ himself. The
means by which people participate in the tradition is
sharing in the receiving and passing on of Christ. When the
end and goal of the action is completed, Christ will hand
himself and all things back to God (Matthew 24:14; I
Corinthians 15:24–28).

The understanding of tradition as God's handing over
Christ to all generations and nations is another key concept
in the work of liberation theologies. It serves to underline
the importance of the biblical promises of liberation by
pointing to the dynamic power of God's action in the world.
God has acted and is acting on behalf of humankind to
break open the established structures. Those who are
oppressed look to this continued action as the basis of their
memory of hope. In the past God has broken into history to
liberate people from themselves and their historical situation. It is this tradition as mission that takes up the central
theme of a usable past, pointing toward hope in a future
which God will make usable. It is possible to join God's
process of tradition creating new language and actions
which allow the gospel to be heard as good news for all
generations and nations.

Tradition in liberation theology. The various forms of liberation theology are frequently seen as a threat to tradition by
those who do not wish to see it broken open in new ways.
Looked at from the point of view of confessional structures
this certainly appears to be true. Liberation theology says
they need to be challenged when they perpetuate a past
which is unusable to a particular group of Christians. For

example they restrict a woman's role at the altar and consider her unable to preside at the sacrament of the Lord's Supper, because of the prohibitions against blood which render a woman "unclean" because of her biological functions.

When tradition is thought of as a deposit of faith which has to be guarded, liberation theology also poses a threat. Yet there is ample biblical evidence to show that it was only later in the New Testament that this static idea of tradition emerged (Jude 1:3; I Timothy 6:20).[31] From its root meaning of *paradosis*, tradition is not a block of static things to be carefully guarded by authorized hierarchies, but a dynamic action of God's love which is to be passed on to others of all sexes and races.

As God's mission extending Christ's love to all people, tradition is not in the least threatened by liberation theologies. Their purpose is to make that love known as God's will to bring liberation, justice, peace and reconciliation to all creation. Because God continues to be actively present in the world through tradition, women and men are set free to share in that action by handing the tradition over to others rather than guarding it for one small group. In this sense liberation theology stands as a reminder that the dynamic of God's tradition transcends and judges all human traditions and actions. Nor does liberation theology stand in the way of tradition as a structural element of human existence. Its very methodology makes use of the dynamic of a still living and evolving past in order to shape a usable future.

There are inherent dangers in liberation theology. It is sometimes very difficult to be faithful to tradition because of many experiences of the misuse of tradition in church and society. Often the tradition that has been carried forward turns out to be useless to those who have been excluded from participation in shaping their own future. The misuse of tradition to legitimatize the rights and privileges of a white, Western, male majority leads to polemical distortion of tradition. Such misuse of tradition to create new forms of legitimatization and polemics should be avoided.

It is not necessary for Third World people and women who are Christians to develop a new religion and create new gods in order to liberate themselves. A return to pre-biblical nature religions, or insistence on a God who is literally black or female is not a necessary part of liberation theology, although it may be helpful in a process of building up self-identity. Rather than abandoning the biblical faith of our forefathers and foremothers, liberation theology has the opportunity to mine the riches of the faith by becoming radical. Radicals are those who penetrate to the root of the matter. In this case it is possible to recover the true meaning of tradition as God's sending of Christ and look to Christ's power to be present in struggling to speak and act the good news in the present and future.

The action-reflection methodology of liberation theology can be a valuable asset in searching out the usable past that can help to shape the future. Out of the reflection on tradition in the light of concrete situations come new models of thought and action. Such a methodology does not lead liberation theology away from the basic *paradosis*, but helps us continue the liberating action of God's mission in the world. This opens the way for the discovery of the presence of the living tradition and sets people free to take risks in shaping the future.

These are challenging times for everyone, including theologians. The time is *now* to enter the struggle for meaning and authentic human existence as we bring to bear all the resources of tradition on the situation of our strife-torn world. In the midst of our actions against oppression and reflection on the meaning of these actions in the light of the liberating message of the gospel, feminist theology and other liberation theologies can provide one of the clues needed as we press toward God's promised future of justice and liberation for all humanity.

Notes

1. Henry S. Commager, "The Search for a Usable Past," *American Heritage*, XVI:2 (February, 1965). Cited by Martin Marty, *The Search for a Usable Future* (New York: Harper and Row, 1969), p. 12.

2. "The Fourth World Manifesto," *Notes from the Third Year: Women's Liberation*, Anne Koedt and Shulamith Firestone (eds.), (P.O. Box AA, Old Chelsea Station, New York, 10011, 1972), p. 118.

3. Jürgen Moltmann, "Political Theology," *Theology Today* (April, 1971), pp. 8–23; cf. J. Metz, "Political Theology," *Sacramentum Mundi* (Herder, 1970), V, 34–38; D. Sölle, *Political Theology* (Philadelphia: Fortress, 1974); C. Clark Chapman, Jr., "Black Theology and Theology of Hope: What Have They To Say To Each Other?," *Union Seminary Quarterly Review*, 29:2 (Winter, 1974), pp. 107–130; M. Douglas Meeks, *Origins of The Theology of Hope* (Philadelphia: Fortress, 1974); Joseph Petulla, *Christian Political Theology: A Marxian Guide* (Maryknoll, New York: Orbis, 1972).

4. J. C. Hoekendijk, *The Church Inside Out* (Philadelphia: Westminster, 1966), p. 79; Thomas Aquinas, "Scientia Conclusionum," *Religion in Geschichte und Gegenwart* (3rd ed., 1972), VI, 777.

5. Rosemary Ruether, *Liberation Theology* (New York: Paulist, 1972), p. 3.

6. William Jones, "Toward An Interim Assessment of Black Theology," *Reflection* 69:2 (January, 1972).

7. Rubem Alves, *A Theology of Human Hope* (Washington: Corpus, 1969), pp. 85–100; James Cone, "The Social Context of Theology: Freedom, History and Hope," *RISK*, 9:2 (1973), pp. 11–33.

8. Jürgen Moltmann, *Hope and Planning* (New York: Harper and Row, 1965), pp. 178–184.

9. Dorothee Sölle, "The Gospel and Liberation," *Commonweal* (22 December 1972), p. 270.

10. Paulo Freire, *Pedagory of the Oppressed* (New York: Herder, 1970), p. 72.

11. Joseph A. Johnson, Jr., "Jesus, the Liberator," *Quest For A Black Theology*, edited by James J. Gardiner and J. Deotis Roberts (Philadelphia: Pilgrim, 1972), pp. 108–111.

12. James Cone, *A Black Theology of Liberation* (Philadelphia: Lippincott, 1970), pp. 186–196.

13. Sölle, *op. cit.*, p. 273.

14. Dorothy L. Sayers, *Are Women Human?* (Grand Rapids: Eerdmans, 1971), pp. 37–47.

15. Some of these publications are: Rosemary Ruether, *Liberation Theology*; Ruether, ed., *Religion and Sexism: Images of Women in Jewish and Christian Tradition* (New York: Simon and Schuster, 1974); Mary Daly, *Beyond God the Father: Toward a Philosophy of Women's Liberation* (Boston: Beacon, 1973); Alice Hageman, ed., *Sexist Religion and Women in the Church: No More Silence* (New York: Association, 1974); Eric Mount, *The Feminine Factor* (Richmond: John Knox, 1973); Letty M. Russell, *Human Liberation in a Feminist Perspective—A Theology* (Philadelphia: Westminster, 1974).

16. *Women Exploring Theology at Grailville, 1972* (Church Women United, New York, N.Y., 10027).

17. One example of this was *Women's Liberation in a Biblical Perspective* by Letty M. Russell (Concern/National Board, YWCA, 1971), which was written as a result of the work of 40 pilot study groups across the country.

18. *Women Exploring Theology at Grailville, 1972.*

19. Nelle Morton, "The Rising Woman Consciousness in a Male Language Structure," *Andover Newton Quarterly* 12:4 (March, 1972), pp. 177–190.

20. Letty M. Russell, *Human Liberation in a Feminist Perspective— A Theology*, Chapter III, "Search for a Usable Past."

21. This sort of tendency can be seen in Mary Daly, *Beyond God The Father*.

22. Burris, *loc. cit.*; Cellestine Ware, *Woman Power* (Tower, 1970), V, 98; Burleigh B. Gardiner, "The Awakening of the Blue Collar Woman," *Intellectual Digest* (March, 1974), p. 17.

23. An attempt is being made to include the world dimension of women's experience through the World Council of Churches, cf. "Sexism in the 1970's," Consultation of women from the six continents, *RISK* (December, 1974, WCC, Geneva).

24. Ruether, *Liberation Theology*, pp. 1–7.

25. Marty, *loc. cit.*

26. *The Problem of Historicity* (Philadelphia: Fortress, 1967), pp. 37–45.

27. Letty M. Russell, "Tradition as Mission," *Study Encounter*, 6:2 (1970), pp. 1–63.

28. Minear, *op. cit.*, pp. 18–19.

29. Peter Lengsfeld, *Überlieferung* (Paderborn: Bonifacius-Druckerei, 1960), p. 28.

30. Oscar Cullmann, "The Tradition," *The Early Church*, edited by A. I. B. Higgins (Philadelphia: Westminster, 1956), pp. 60, 70–72.

31. Josef Geiselmann, *The Meaning of Tradition* (New York: Herder, 1966), p. 23.

American Indian Religion and Religio-Cultural Identity

CARL F. STARKLOFF

Religion is not lived by people because it functions as a social or psychological healer. With religious analysts like William James and Joachim Wach, I believe that religion exists as an integral part of human spirit. In cultures permeated with religious symbols the suppression of traditional religious expression is catastrophic. In this essay, I would like to explore the truth of that thesis in regard to the Native American culture.

Support for this position is widespread. Shortly before the beginnings of the current outcry for ethnic identity in North America, a joint economic committee of the United States Congress made the following statement in a study of Native American social and economic problems:

> The strong federal and missionary attacks on the ancient religions, regardless of what may have seemed necessary in the late nineteenth and early twentieth centuries for suppressing pagan, obscene or torture elements of Indian customs, had a destructive effect in undermining the system of ideas and moral order that gave cohesion and stability to the tribal life. There has followed the spread of the so-called peyote cult to replace the old religion with a new form

comprised of old religious symbols and customs and directed toward the personal problems, unhappiness, and ill health of its adherents. Acceptance of this cult is far from universal, but it appears to grow as it soothes present psychological anxieties and fills a need for an Indian-rooted belief system.[1]

In 1973, a research team of the National Institute of Mental Health found these reasons for the high incidence of suicide, homicide and alcoholism among American Indians: cultural identity conflicts, loss of tradition and heritage, prejudice and discrimination, movement away from spiritual interests, and peer group pressures among adolescents. Political factors such as governmental paternalism and a dominant society inhibiting self-expression, decision-making and control of individual destiny were contributors as well as environmental factors. Here the committee simply cites the bare facts of both reservation and urban life of American Indians.[2]

Last winter I attended a local meeting of university social scientists and scholars with representatives of urban and rural Indian groups. We were called there to discuss ways of helping local Indian people in the direction of economic and social self-determination. After some discussion of possibilities for obtaining political and financial independence, one of the tribal leaders rather startled the group—including me, the clergyman—when he opened his talk by insisting on the importance of religion in Indian politics, on the respect for the Creator in the way we use or misuse His gifts. "State and Church," he said, "are the same to Indians." He did not mean to support an established church, but to impress upon his audience that reverence and piety and religious symbolism profoundly affect social conduct. After this, there arose, while I chose to remain silent, an animated discussion of whether American Indian religion could be said to be implicitly Christian or not!

We should not be too surprised at this aspect of the

liberation movement. After all, even Harvey Cox has led his pilgrimage caravan into the territory, not of the secular but of the sacred, and now voices a loud *nostra culpa* (I *hope* he includes himself) for what intellectuals have done to "people's religion." Desacralization, it has become clear, may lead us prophetically away from abuses perpetrated in the name of sacred figures and privileged persons, but the idea of the holy haunts us all the more the farther we wander from the holy place. It would seem that it is "the holy" which now pricks the conscience of American government, under the traditional American pragmatic rubric, for its clumsy handling of Indian rites and customs peremptorily termed "obscene" or "savage." Sadly enough, the same spectre torments the churches who forced Indians to disenchant nature, to desacralize politics, and to deconsecrate their values. These same churches, apparently unwittingly, superimposed on Indians an Italian, English, Spanish or French cultural religious form. Such a joint cooperation of religion and monarch, and the response to it, is not new to those who read the First Book of Maccabees.

Thus the intimate and delicate relationship between faith, religion and culture, and the threat posed to human freedom by insensitive handling of these, is the theme of this essay. I propose to consider the theses of Paul Tillich on the delicate balance of religion and culture, with observations on the rooting of faith within a given culture, and to show Indian liberation is a religious movement. As I refer to the work of contemporary Indian intellectuals, I fully realize that I may be risking a cooperation in the obsequies of Indian Christianity. The close harmony between religion and culture will be illustrated by more significant examples of the effect on Indian life of religious values and symbols. Finally, I will cautiously propose suggestions for churches and religious educators in their efforts to find a holiness that is also, to use Goldbrunner's phrase, wholeness—and therefore liberation.

Relationship between Religion and Culture

In many of his writings, Paul Tillich has contended that religion is the substance of culture and culture is the form of religion[3]—these two and a third, morality, are essentially related in the unity of spirit. This principle, brought out in detail by religious sociologists like Wach and religious phenomenologists like Ninian Smart, is necessitated by modern, reflective and secularized society. The so-called "primitive societies" would never occupy themselves with this problem or think of these areas as unrelated. Whatever the drawbacks to such a primitive mentality, we see here the fact that faith—even the transcendent faith-commitment of a Kierkegaard or a Karl Barth—must have a culture in which to live. Tillich's warnings against religion's controlling culture or culture's engulfing religion[4] point out to us the problem of Christian missionary efforts within primitive societies. When the churches proclaimed Jesus Christ to Indian tribes, they seemed on the surface to be controlling a culture in the name of religion. But was it not more likely the other way around? Was it not likely that various national cultures, transplanted in the name of Christianity, were actually engulfing many valid *religious* experiences as expressed through primitive culture? Was it, for example, his faith or his social training that led one missionary of my acquaintance to tell Indians involved in the Sun Dance that they were "dancing themselves to hell"?

The response to this problem is not a simple one, but we might find some guidance, both for primitive societies and for "modern" Christians, in Tillich's definition of culture: "Culture, *cultura,* is that which takes care of something, keeps it alive, and makes it grow," [5] through that culture's language and other means of cultivation. A summation of Tillich's position is that culture provides the contents of morality, while religion gives to morality the unconditional character of the moral imperative, and to culture the "inexhaustible depth of a genuine creation." [6] These three functions of life under the dimension of spirit are unified in what Tillich calls, using Hegelian language, the state of "dreaming innocence." There is no independent culture in dreaming innocence—a state we might attribute to primitive tribal society before the arrival of "Western civilization." With Tillich, we must indeed grant that life itself is based on our losing this dreaming innocence and experiencing the ambiguities based on rational reflection. And yet, as Tillich points out, this mediacy is a state of alienation (as we all witness in our faith crises and intellectualization of faith), and synthesis must be sought all over again. If religion, morality and culture all contribute in some way to our sense of the self-transcendent, the ultimate, then theologians and other scholars stand under the mandate to respect both the unity and the independence of these three dimensions. What is involved here is humanity's search for meaningful symbols—a search engaged in with great passion even by secularized man becoming conscious of his own inner depths.

But what about the society that is, even today, experiencing many elements of the primitive unity of spirit? Suppose the symbols, myths and rituals of a tribe still express genuine ultimacy and religious validity? Must Christianity then be the destruction of these symbols, or might it live within them or the more universal of them, and lead their possessors to further transcendent life? The function of faith, as expressed by the more radical neo-orthodox position for example, is to issue a resounding "No!" to all natural theology as a "way of salvation." And yet, by the very principles of this same moment, no culture of itself is a way of salvation apart from the Word of God. Might not this transcendental faith find its expression in and through countless cultures?

Indian Liberation as a Religious Movement

A vehement rejection of this possibility is now the consistent theme of Vine Deloria, Jr. who in his latest book, *God Is Red*, renounces what has come to be seen by many as the very essence of Christianity. He rejects the linear, historical nature of Christianity, denies the possibility of any religion's transcending its original environment, and denounces the Christian witness to monotheism. And how could he do otherwise? Here are Deloria's reasons, to which I suggest you listen in the light of prevalent pastoral and theological attitudes and actual American frontier history.

Linear time concepts, says Deloria, form an ideology that sparked the Crusades, the Age of Exploration, the Age of Imperialism and Nationalism, as well as the recent crusade against communism.[7] The theology behind such thinking is the salvation history that begins with creation, experiences alienation when Adam and Eve disobey God, progresses through time with the Chosen People of Abraham and Moses, culminates in Jesus Christ, and will attain realization at the end of time.[8] Although there is alienation from nature in man, his redemption in Christ promises that history will justify Christian faith as it spreads throughout the world. After all, Deloria notes sarcastically Christian progress in Europe found one of its strongest historical supports in the growth of the Heavenly City of the Thousand Year Reich! [9] In modern secularization theology, God leads His people to their destiny through social change as found in the Secular City. Whatever one's views of the historicity of biblical events, God's message is that man must be uprooted from all cultural ties. Deloria quotes Harvey Cox's *The Secular City*: ". . . tribal naivete must be laid to rest everywhere, and everyone must be made a citizen of the land of broken symbols." [10] While Deloria is being unfair to Cox here, charging him with the very intolerance Cox was trying to denounce, there is little doubt that Cox *was* viewing tribal religion simplistically and undervaluing the sacral basis of morality. It is very easy for a Christian secularist of lesser breadth of vision than Cox to conclude that whatever stands in the way of Christian progress must go under.

This transcendence of environment that follows upon the Christian idea of history is nothing more than suicide to a religion, says Deloria. We see this today as American expressions of Christianity result in nothing but chaos—vulgar expressions without roots or tradition that style themselves "liturgy" or worship, the susceptibility to absorb the values of a decadent profane society because there are no values rooted in a sacred homeland. "The world in which Christianity arose no longer exists in its social and political sense . . . The question is whether the modern world can have any valid religious experiences or knowledge whatsoever." [11]

Monotheism too, however "logically pleasing," is destructive to the experience of wholeness and oneness with the universe, and leads its adherents to look upon "their" God as He who leads them into battle against their enemies.[12] Aside from the fact that experience does not necessarily support monotheism, as a doctrine it is destructive because it depends on a revelation given at a point in historical time that must then validate itself at points throughout history and around the planet, even while the "gods of the land" constantly raise their heads in revolt.[13] To think that one personal God subdues all the other spirits in this world is to create a radical discontinuity between man and the world of his most intimate experience. Sin, for monotheism, is the breaking of this deity's laws, leading man to ignore the laws already built into nature itself, which need no one divine lawgiver to enforce or proclaim them. Death, consequently, is an object of fear to Christians, paradoxically, because it not only symbolizes radical discontinuity with the world but is a sign of God's punishment for the breaking of laws. To the tribal mentality, on the contrary, death is a simple reality of natural process.

However many arguments we may find in rebuttal to this thorough strafing of our theological battle stations—and no doubt some of the charges are unfair—my point here is that the present condition of this "Christian nation" verifies such arguments. American history itself, as more facts come to light, shows that the churches have often been the tools of imperialism. The deeply moving book of Cheyenne Hyemeyohsts Storm, *Seven Arrows*,[14] will horrify the white reader as it describes how Indian people experienced the onslaught of the frontier, and the abuse of unscrupulous adventurers, who used the names of God and Jesus as supernatural allies supporting their own personal ambitions—a use the Indian can well understand, in his concept of religion as supernatural "power."

That the theories heretofore discussed have been involved in many of the more tragic aspects of Christian-Indian relationships is evident to those who spend time on reservations or with urban Indian groups. We have already mentioned the crisis of alcoholism. However much missionaries and clergy may be able to help some Indians to battle problems with drink by means of counselling or Alcoholics Anonymous, the roots of the problem—probably the same roots as it has been in white society, if we can believe experts like Howard Clinebell—lie in the alienation from any familiar way of experiencing oneness with the universe and with God as He is understood. The shockingly high incidence of suicide among young Indians may with good support be attributed to rootlessness and lack of identity. Among many tribes too, a strong "rugged individualism," generally supported by both Catholic and Protestant church people, tends to replace inbuilt systems of social equity based on tribal religious customs. What has been called the Protestant ethic finds its reflection in many Indians who now enter the competitive market against their fellow tribespeople—a phenomenon found rarely in primitive cultures. The conflict between Indian sacred time with its accompanying lack of concern for chronological time, and the timeclocks of white employers living adjacent to reservations, is already well-known.

I am not trying to impute all the causes of this malaise to white Christianity; Indian tribes were not and are not communities full of saints with entirely noble social and religious customs. And very often Indians do find in Christianity the strength to lead devout, charitable and constructive lives. My point here is that this same Christianity might be more real to more Indians if it would re-examine its ways of expressing itself. The liberating power of God in Christ should certainly not be obscured by the distortions so often shown to Native Americans. But before this liberation from sin and death can be realized, the more concrete tyranny of cultural vacuum and rootlessness must be dethroned. To borrow from Reinhold Niebuhr, while individuals might experience conversion and arrive at freedom independently of cultural ties, the collective is not dealt with as simply. It needs the environment of mythological and cultural warmth in order to grow.

Sacred Space and Community

With this argument in mind, I wish to point out a number of "primal" religious experiences basic to Indian culture, which have profound effects on social and personal freedom. In so doing, I am making the suggestion that derivatives of such experiences are archetypically valid for healing many of the ills of American religion and society.

Vine Deloria describes the Indian view of creation, in contrast with the linear view of creation as a moment in time. Creation is, to the Indian, "an ecosystem present in a definable place." [15] The oldest Indian stories show the Creator giving the tribe its place to live in, and the tribe naming it "the center of the earth." The theme of "sacred space" dominates most, if not all, Indian world views. Even the reservation land to which tribes have been forcibly moved is seen as a sacred dwelling-place. One plains tribe even now has its reservation land bounded by four shrines at the four points of the compass.

The loss of a sense of place is an obvious catastrophe for Native Americans, but it has its impact on all of us. Ecologists have drummed into us the urgency of developing respect for this "ecosystem" that sustains our lives. But I shall not dwell on the obvious. The environment of life touches the human spirit as well: as Eliade tells us, no one becomes so secularized that he completely loses the religious longing for the "holy places" of his private universe, a universe where he has an ordered world, a cosmos set apart from chaos.[16] Defend as we must the God-given power to transcend the literal place we occupy on this globe, what society has ever been able to rear and educate its children in a state of rootless mobility? Educators today, especially religious educators, are insisting on a healthy and life-sustaining environment of training as necessary for reaching maturity. As I find myself thinking how to carry out authentic religious education programs among Indian people as well as among my own students, I realize more and more strongly that I am constructing in my mind a milieu for education in a parish or church congregation—a "belonging" knit together by meaningful symbols and myths, a community that offers strength to its members as they confront the chaos of external society where there is little respect for the person as such. When ecclesiologists today speak of the local church as exercising so profound an influence on the lives of Christians, their basic model in the study of religious archetypes would seem to be that of "sacred space."

Closely related to the center of the world and sacred space notions is the Indian view of the individual as a measure of the cosmos. The plains Indian image, described so well by H. B. Alexander, of the skeletal frame of man centered within the meeting point of the Four Winds, head to the heavens and feet upon the earth, expresses a mystic vision of the centeredness of each human person in his universe. It is a centeredness ultimately realized only through discipline, suffering, prayer. It is the spiritual basis of all moral and social integrity. Even within the sadly shattered life of Indian tribes today, Indian people seek to experience this integrity and to express it ritually. The Sun Dance of the plains tribes, with analogies among tribes of other areas, is social in its religious symbolism. The worshippers suffer "for the people," just as in the Peyote Tipi one finds the center of many a reformed and redirected personal life. The various Green Corn Dances, the Algon-quian-Delaware Big House, and the many still-extant rites of passage are symbols effecting social and individual wholeness. As one observes contemporary forms of such rites, an intimate relationship between worship and social welfare is evident. The elaborate gift-giving still carried on ritually by so many tribes is no sentimental altruism which ultimately demeans its recipients. Rather, gift-giving ac-cording to traditional Indians, is assurance of an exchange in equity when one might need it; or it can be another form of social unity, in which competitive gift-giving replaces more violent forms of confrontation.

It is the disappearance of such possibilities of exchange and growth that constitutes enslavement, leading to a loss of personal dignity and social integrity. Can society today find the means to restore such integrity without the use of rites, symbols and worship? Listening to the jeremiads of social critics and reading the newspapers, one might well doubt it. Whatever theological and psychological criticism may be levelled at Karl Menninger's call for a return to the sense of sin in social life, we might well ask ourselves if the root of social ills is not religious.

Transformation of Sin and Death

The possibility of a positive answer to this question brings us to reflect on the "sense of sin" discussed earlier in relation to Deloria's book. If modern man can think of God only in the simplistic form of law-giver, of sin as breaking those laws, and death as His punishing hand, he will never experience the wholeness offered by a deeper look into both primitive religion and Christian theology.

In his famous work, *On The Theology of Death*, Karl Rahner, who derives his ideas largely from Martin Heidegger, proposes a view of sin, death, and the world and our relationship to it that strikingly resembles the mystic understanding of primal Indian religion. Rahner would have us contemplate death on its spiritual and moral levels, as a religious experience qualitatively different from a mere body-soul dissolution. The soul has, through its substantial union with the body, a relationship to the radical oneness of the universe. The human spirit is not a-cosmic, "out of the world," but related to it through a deeper, all-embracing openness—a "transcendental relationship" to matter.[17] Rahner places the human spirit in the category of "life-entelechies" related to the ultimate, meta-empirical grounds of material existence. Thus, when the soul passes from its role of giving life to the body, it takes on as it were, a new body in the world as a whole. The soul is then all-cosmic, not as the one soul of the universe obviously, but insofar as the soul has a definite determining personal effect on the universe, and the universe on the soul.[18] After death the relationship is realized, even as it is experienced in the moral relationship each individual always has with the world in which he exists.

Both sin and death, in this light, have a deep cosmological significance. Sin is the refusal to live this radical oneness with the created universe; it is the rejection of it as the God-given sphere of my existence, and a closing-off of my potential unity with God, man and universe—the object of existence for Indian religion. When I sin, I do grave harm to myself, my relation to God, to my neighbor or the universe; I damage or destroy the radical harmony of all these relationships. To view sin as simply a violation of law is to elevate law to an absolute position, and the diety of "monotheism" in this light is a deity who as such has no relationship with the universe. He becomes the god of Aristotelianism, not the God of revelation who places himself in rapport with His creatures. For Rahner, death is an event-decision in which, throughout life, I ratify my relationship with the cosmos, either by enriching it or destroying it. The moment of biological death is the final symbolic act of that life-long event, such as we witness in the death chants of warriors of the plains.

If we could experience Indian myths and customs dealing with death, we would find, I believe, not an absence of sin, as some anthropologists have indicated, but the primitive foundation of a profound theological analysis of sin and death. According to John Bryde, the Indian of tradition sees his life-goal to be harmony within himself, and with God, fellow-man and the universe.[19] Every rite performed and myth narrated is in some way centered on the development of these relationships or repairing them if broken. The Eastern Algonquin peoples see humanity living in a World House; if a person acts to sully or damage that house, he destroys the harmony of life and impairs his own relationship to life. In other words the contemplative view of the universe, seemingly so ethereal, is the most practical and earthy of all viewpoints. If humanity cannot return to a past age of "dreaming innocence," in which religion, morality and culture are identical, it must maintain or recover as much of the basic harmony among the three as human nature will allow.

We as Christians are well-advised to consider Deloria's

condemnation of Judeo-Christian historicism. It is important to reformulate our sense of history, both from theory and from praxis—"action . . . under the dimension of spirit," as Tillich defined it.[20] We must develop our theology of history, of the Incarnation and of the role of faith within culture, and we must *do* the very things about which we speculate, developing a theology of cultural identity.

Historicism as the crude notion of progressive desacralization is ultimately foreign to the Bible. However much the worship of the One God deprives idols of their divine power, never does there have to be a discarding of the sacred as a special dimension of life, and of the overall sense of the world as holy. Rather, theology must take the notion of *historicity,* of the Word incarnated in the world and within a given culture, as an essential element of liberation. Never denying that Christian faith is transcendent of cultures, we must know that it is nurtured within a culture and expressed by cultural forms. A delicate balance between establishing a universal rubric and accepting local symbols must be maintained. We, after all, cannot appreciate the meaning of Incarnation until we have seen what it meant for Jesus, the Rabbi from Galilee, as well as what it means within a context in the present day.

To return to the comments of my Pottawotomi friend, mentioned at the beginning of this essay, Native Americans have always been incapable of seeing a religious act as asocial or apolitical, or a social or political act as non-religious. Politico-social praxis then is already at work in religious observance: in the gift-giving so essential at Sun Dance rites, in the exchange of articles of food at religious meals, in the ratifying of agreements at a pipe-ceremony. What we do for the sake of harmony is done for the Creator. But even more deeply, and really more simply, the whole thesis of this essay is that a person who can worship, truly worship, is already a free person, paradoxically capable of transcending those very forms that nurture him when he decides that it is necessary.

Local or tribal religion alone is not sufficient, but if the gods of the land and tribal deities are not destroyed by the One God, they are at least His messengers. Tribal forms of worship do have an importance, and the integration of these with basic Christian worship is not only possible but essential. The churches will have to be ready to take the risks involved in experimenting with these forms. Perhaps an example from my personal experience will illustrate the freedom already being realized by this reviving sense of identity. When I first attended the Arapaho Sun Dance in 1970, breaking a taboo in existence for decades, the Indian reaction was a combination of surprise and pleasure, that maybe now the Church was recognizing the possibility of Indians being both Christian and following the old religion in its modern forms. When I attended again in 1972, I was invited to give three opening invocations at the Sunrise Ceremonies, and was requested to let people know that all this "was really O.K." When I attended in 1973, the Episcopal bishop was invited to say the opening night invocation as a gesture of friendship, but no one was asked to pray at sunrise. The dance itself and the cries of the holy man were enough. There was no hostility here, but simply a sense of progressively knowing where they were going. As I stood one evening at the entrance to the Sun Dance Offerings Lodge, talking with a young Arapaho woman who had been a pupil of mine and was now a trained social worker, I remarked that the days of Church condemnation of things Indian were drawing to a close. Without any bitterness at all she replied, "I'm glad to hear that, Father, because it wouldn't make much difference anyway."

Notes

1. Joint Economic Committee, Congress of the United States,

American Indians: Facts and Future (New York: Arno Press, 1970), p. 63.

2. National Institute of Mental Health, *Suicide, Homicide and Alcoholism Among American Indians: Guidelines for Help* (Washington, D.C.: U.S. Government Printing Office, 1973), pp. 29ff.

3. See, for example, Paul Tillich, *Systematic Theology* (Chicago: Chicago University Press, 1963), III, pp. 248–249.

4. *Ibid.*, p. i4.

5. *Ibid.*, p. 57.

6. *Ibid.*, p. 95.

7. Vine Deloria, Jr., *God Is Red* (New York: Grossett and Dunlap, 1973), p. 76.

8. *Ibid.*, ch. 7.

9. *Ibid.*, p. 115.

10. *Ibid.*, p. 201. Deloria quotes Cox inaccurately. Cf. Harvey Cox, *The Secular City* (New York: Macmillan, 1966), p. 31.

11. *Ibid.*, p. 244.

12. *Ibid.*, p. 292.

13. *Ibid.*, p. 80.

14. Hyemeyohsts Storm, *Seven Arrows* (New York: Ballantine Books, 1972).

15. Deloria, *op. cit.*, p. 91.

16. Mircea Eliade, *The Sacred and the Profane*, trans. Willard R. Trask (New York: Harper and Row, 1961), p. 28ff.

17. Karl Rahner, *On the Theology of Death* (New York: Herder and Herder, 1961), pp. 27–28.

18. *Ibid.*, p. 30.

19. John R. Bryde, *Acculturational Psychology or Modern Indian Psychology* (United States Department of the Interior, Bureau of Indian Affairs, 1967), pp. 7–8.

20. Tillich, *op. cit.*, p. 66.

Freedom in Roman Catholicism and Zen Buddhism: a study in inter-religious dialogue

SILVIO E. FITTIPALDI

Human persons exist in a given situation. They are born with a given nature into a given world, society and culture. This context cannot be denied, and seems so to bind us into its rhythm that freedom from it appears merely hypothetical. Yet it is within our condition that freedom can be attained. The purpose of this essay is to discuss the nature of this freedom.

An initial distinction will be of value to us. Freedom is often understood to deal with choice. But when choice is so limited that freedom seems impossible, freedom becomes a matter of attitude. Freedom is also understood as freedom of being, and is described by the Roman Catholic theologian, Karl Rahner, as the very ground of freedom—more basic than freedom of choice and attitude. It is also the center of the Zen search for a condition that is unconditioned. This paper will struggle with the issue of freedom and necessity by presenting insights from both the Roman Catholic and Zen Buddhist traditions.

There is a Zen story that points to the various approaches to freedom suggested above, freedom of choice, freedom of attitude and freedom of being. A young man was walking through a forest on a sunny afternoon when suddenly he was attacked by a tiger. The man began to run as fast as he could. The tiger was gaining on him. The man ran faster. He reached the edge of the forest and ran into an open field. The tiger came closer. The field became shorter and shorter and the young man came to an abyss. He could not go to the right or to the left. The tiger was approaching quickly. The only path the man could take was over the edge. Over he went, grasping onto a vine. Hanging onto the vine the man could not go up. The tiger was waiting for him above. He looked down and just below him there was another tiger waiting for him to fall. Not being able to go up or to go down the young man noticed two mice nibbling away at the vine. Caught in mid-air, hanging onto a vine that was gradually being weakened, with a tiger above him and a tiger below him, the young man noticed a strawberry within his reach. He stretched out, picked it and ate it. He then exclaimed, "How tasty!"

Freedom of Choice

The young man in the story suddenly found himself in an unexpected situation. He had a few choices which were limited by his situation and by his own resources: he could run away, climb a tree, or stand and fight the tiger. Freedom is predominantly understood to be this freedom of choice. Thus a person is free if he is able to walk into a store to buy what is needed or desired. The choices, however, are limited by what the store has in stock. A person is also considered free if he can live in a desired neighborhood, but this choice also is limited by the homes and sites available. A person is considered free if he can become educated in a desired discipline or work at a desired job. Here the choice is limited by the skill and/or the intellectual potential of the person, as well as by the openings in the work force or school. Thus choices are defined opportunities having to do with money, personal skill or cultural structures. However, even if one's choices are limited, the person strives to increase the quality of choices and their quantity. The young man who was running away from the tiger did have a choice as to what he could do when he was attacked. He did not, however, choose that the tiger attack him at that moment.

This type of freedom, a finite freedom of choice, is defined by Karl Rahner:

> Finite freedom of choice . . . is a choice which is imposed on us without our being able to choose it ourselves. It is a choice, imposed without choice, which can itself be the least free of all if the scope given to it, and within which it is exercised, is itself already a prison of bondage in the wrong place—somewhat as if one were to say to someone sitting in a prison cell that he is free, because he can choose in which corner of his dungeon he wishes to sit. Everything depends on the object of one's freedom.[1]

Thus freedom of choice is dependent on the situation out of which the choices are made. There is a great degree of unfreedom in the freedom of choice.

Freedom of choice is also often related to freedom of the will. It is popularly understood that when some choices are presented to a person, the person inspects these choices rationally and then, using his will, decides which choice to make. Maturity or adulthood then consists of freely doing what should be done and freely refraining from doing what should not be done. This freedom is described by the Japanese Zen Buddhist philosopher Shin-ichi Hisamatsu who suggests that "aspiration to such rational freedom is characteristically human."[2] Yet Hisamatsu suggests that even this rational freedom is dependent on the choices that are available.

To suggest that a human person becomes a human

person in terms of the choices and decisions he makes is to say that the ordinary person becomes a person in the realm of unfreedom. Ultimately this means that freedom is not a fundamental characteristic of the becoming human person. How could it be if the very choices or decisions that the human person makes are dependent upon what is available? In the end, the person does not create self but rather is created in terms of the possibilities that are present in the choices that are available. Thus when Rahner states that "everything depends on the object of one's freedom" he points out the poignancy of the fundamental unfreedom which confronts all of us. We are not unlike the prisoner who can choose what corner he sits in, but does not choose the prison cell.

In Zen this unfreedom belies the duality of the human condition according to both D. T. Suzuki and Hisamatsu.[3] There are many forms of this duality: self and other, self and not self, life and death, body and mind, freedom and destiny. It must be recognized, however, that freedom is intrinsically bound up with the others and that each duality simply expresses the fundamental subject-object duality of the human situation.

The duality of freedom and destiny is manifested in freedom of choice. In this choice the human being realizes that there is a distinction between himself and that which is to be chosen or not chosen. The human being also finds himself determined by the possible choices that can be made. Thus the ordinary human being is dualistically constituted as both act and as fact. He is act insofar as he chooses from this or that. He is fact insofar as the choices available are already given. It is as act that the ordinary human determines himself, but it is the already existing fact that establishes the course of this "self-determination." These two dimensions of the human situation are interdependent. "Free choice" is determined by the choices that are available. On the other hand, our power to choose allows the *de facto* range of choices to be operative. For if the human did not have the power of choice, the fact that there were or were not a number of choices would not make any difference. This situation itself is the condition of the duality of freedom and destiny.

This differentiation between the ordinary human and the objects of choice is at the root of the unfreedom of the ordinary human. These objects of choice may be considered to be the form which a choice may take. This "form" of the ordinary human is precisely its limitation. Hisamatsu writes:

> Our ordinary self, because differentiated, necessarily has some kind of form; and the condition of its having form limits it. Thus being limited, it is restricted and bound, and is deprived of its freedom.[4]

This unfreedom of the ordinary human becomes even clearer in the following statement by Hisamatsu:

> The ordinary "I" therefore, is an "I" which is always connected with an object. . . . Such an "I" is an "I" which can not but be limited by color when seeing color, by sound when hearing sound, by evil when thinking of evil, and by good when thinking of good. It is an "I" which is always limited and captured by the "internal" and "external" realms, that is, by objects.[5]

Hisamatsu further points out the unfreedom of ordinary human freedom of choice when he writes, with many examples, of the constriction of form that is the limitation of the very condition of the ordinary human:

> To consider some ordinary instances: when we are in health we are determined as being in health and have the form of health; when we are ill we are determined as being ill and

have the form of illness. In life we have the form of life; in death we have the form of death. The rich man has the form of wealth, the poor man has the form of poverty; the person of high status possesses the form of being a scholar, the man of religion possesses the form of being a man of religion. All, consequently, are captured and bound by the forms they possess.

Similarly, in pleasure there is the form of pleasure, in sadness the form of sadness; in anger there is the form of anger, in love the form of love; in hatred there is the form of hatred, in goodness the form of goodness, and in evil the form of evil.

By that which it possesses the self restricts, delimits, and binds itself by its own rope, as it were, and thereby loses its freedom.[6]

Thus freedom of choice which is dependent on the objects available or on the human forms involved turns out again to be unfreedom. It is true that the person is able to choose this or that but the very fact of choosing is bound by what is available, by the form or the condition of the very choice. This situation is recognized by both Roman Catholics and Zen Buddhists.

Freedom of Attitude

Let us return to the situation of the man being chased by a tiger. As he is hanging by a vine, out of reach of the tigers above and below, his position of relative safety is threatened by the two mice eating away at the vine. It might be suggested at this point that while this man has few choices that are truly free, there is another kind of freedom which is not dependent on the situation or on what choices are available. This kind of freedom is spoken of as an inner freedom. It is here where the human being is unassailable. The inner self cannot be determined, it is suggested, by choices that are or are not available. Even though the external conditions may be quite limiting the person can determine his own attitude toward these conditions, and no one and no thing can ultimately determine how the human feels toward the circumstances. Hanging from a gradually weakening vine with death facing him, the man can be free insofar as his inner attitude cannot be ultimately determined by his condition.

It is almost impossible for us to conceive of this kind of freedom. As long as we think of freedom mainly as freedom of choice, we allow our inner attitude to be determined by external conditions. Let us assume that a person is able to transcend the conditions of his concrete situation. In the case of the man in prison, let us assume that he recognizes his plight and retains his inner freedom of attitude toward this plight. Yet even this type of freedom is also quite limited.

Rahner argues that such "inner freedom" is not only limited but that it is not freedom at all. He suggests that this "interior freedom" is totally isolating. Thus the human is a prisoner bound by the limitations of his own nature. This type of freedom would leave us in a futile position. Everything within and without would, then, be alien and oppressive.[7] This type of freedom is also perceived in Zen to be another form of unfreedom. It is another "form." Hisamatsu points out that the ordinary "I" is always limited and captured by internal as well as external realms. Further, in Zen the interior freedom is unfreedom insofar as it is bound up in the duality of inner and outer. In Zen this duality is the source of the anxiety and hence of unfreedom. Thus the Sixth Chinese patriarch of Zen, Hui Neng, has proclaimed: "As long as there is a dualistic way of looking at things, there is no emancipation."[8] True freedom is not the freedom of choice nor is it the freedom of attitude. Both of these types of freedom are fundamentally unfree.

We have seen that the limited creativity of freedom, attributable to the pre-existent conditions which determine choice, is expressive of a fundamental human problem, that is, how a person can really be free in the face of the already given. Rahner responds to this issue saying that it is precisely the human acceptance of the condition of being finite that is essential to the adequate realization of freedom:

> Man always exercises his original freedom towards himself by merely accepting and passing through the history pre-given and imposed on him. Freedom is the free answer of yes or no to necessity and once more experiences in this its created nature.[9]

Thus an essential element of finite freedom is the acceptance of its necessary limitations. This freedom is quite similar to the rational freedom described by Hisamatsu, that is, doing freely what should be done and freely refraining from doing what should not be done. Rahner suggests that there are two ways of accepting the necessary. The first is the attempt to change what, in the necessary, is foreign to the person. The second is the simple acceptance of the foreign element of the necessary. In both cases, the response overcomes the foreignness of the necessary. To accept the necessary is to say yes to it and hence to the ground which itself limits freedom.[10] It is a way of "freely" accepting the nonfreedom of the ordinary human. Another name for this is fate.

This human condition is directly related to the theological concepts of original sin and concupiscence. According to Rahner the doctrines of original sin and concupiscence

> . . . mean that man's freedom finds no situation or material for its own decision that have not already also been partly determined by the guilt of mankind, and till the end of history it will not be possible wholly to eliminate this burden of guilt.[11]

Thus the Christian doctrine of original sin is expressive of the fundamental unfreedom of the ordinary human.

The Freedom of Being

The young man hanging from a vine thus is able to accept his fate and become interiorly free. But this freedom is quite limited. Both Roman Catholicism and Zen Buddhism proclaim that there is another freedom above ordinary human. In Zen this freedom is the emancipation which is enlightenment. In Roman Catholicism it is salvation.

The young man hanging by a vine saw a strawberry, reached out, picked it, ate it and exclaimed: "How tasty!" This man is certainly aware of his own precarious condition. Being confronted in such a manner he could easily be preoccupied with this situation. He could easily be quite anxious. He does not leave his condition; he knows that he cannot. Yet he can enjoy a strawberry. It is not a matter of choice that he enjoy the strawberry or not enjoy it. It is not a matter of his willing to eat and enjoy the fruit. If this were so the young man would not be free, except in the limited senses suggested in the first part of this paper. Nor is the freedom of the young man an interior freedom in which his attitude is one of acceptance of the necessity of the sitatuion which is not allowed to touch his inner being. Rather the young man is free insofar as he is not bound by any forms, the form of life or the form of death, the form of hunger or the form of eating. This is the freedom of Zen, not being constrained by any form. This freedom is not a denial of form. If it were then the condition of the young man would still be one of duality, the duality of form and non-form, and he would still be unfree. Rather the young man would be, in Zen terms, a "man of no title." His situation would be one of non-attachment. This non-attachment is not such that it denies all wordly reality or forms or titles. For there is form and attachment in being one who is non-attached. "Man of no title" can itself be a title. Rather non-attachment means that one can take on any form because of not having any form. One can take on any title. Hisamatsu gives expression to this freedom when he writes:

> Only the Self that, while in the midst of the world, is yet unattached to and free from it is capable of being unrestricted and free in dealing with it. So long as we remain "something," we can never be free. Thus, by being nonattached is meant the freedom to take on any form because of not having form. This freedom, when it is actualized in both what is expressed and what is expressing itself, is also what is meant by non-attachment.[12]

Richard DeMartino, a student of both Suzuki and Hisamatsu, gives expression to this freedom of non-attachment when he describes the true freedom of a wealthy person and the true freedom of a hobo. A wealthy person who depends on his wealth for his identity, for his status, for personal prestige and power is a slave to his wealth. He does not enjoy the freedom of the hobo. But the hobo also may be captured by his state of being a hobo. He may not be free to "not be a hobo." He may be bound by the image of what it means to be a hobo. The hobo would be free if he could not only be one who is unshaven and wear tattered clothes but also dress in a tuxedo at a wedding banquet.[13]

These analogies bring us to the very meaning of freedom in Zen. Freedom is authentic Selfhood. Thus Hisamatsu writes:

> In Buddhism, however, the ultimate is for us to awaken to the Self which, not being bound by anything—not even by its "not being bound"—works freely. Indeed, it will be even more correct to say that just because it is not bound by—or to—anything it can work freely.[14]

In Zen this freedom is called enlightenment. Suzuki points out: "Enlightenment means emancipation. And emancipation is not less than freedom." [15] To be free is to be bound by no form. It is to be the True Self which is not rigid but rather fluid. The fluidity is not bound by form. Thus the freedom of Zen which is enlightenment is also called emptiness. Thus the young man hanging from the vine and enjoying the strawberry is not bound by his condition. Nor is he bound to eat and enjoy the strawberry. His self is not rigidly determined by his precarious position. He is as Hisamatsu writes, "completely unconditioned and non-dependent." He is a truly free subject, that is he has actualized his True Nature.[16]

Thomas Merton, a Trappist monk greatly influenced by Zen during the last ten years of his life, correlates Zen enlightenment (emptiness) with Christian poverty of spirit. He suggests that poverty of spirit is an openness to God in the human. This openness, he points out, is not a preparation of a place for God to act in the human. Rather it is a radical poverty that has no place for God to act. There is, in other words, no form to which the self is bound. Thus the human can be open to the limitless Self who God is.[17] This is also the significance that Merton finds in the central Christian realization of kenosis which, he writes, involves "an emptying of all the contents of the ego-consciousness to become a void in which the light of God or the glory of God, the full radiation of the infinite reality of His Being and Love are manifested." [18]

This kenotic realization, for the Christian, is salvation. It is, as St. Paul writes, "having that mind in you which is in Christ Jesus." [19] The "mind of Christ" is not merely the rational mind nor is it the ego-mind. It is rather the realization of the self-emptying of Christ who was not attached to the divinity but became as humans are. Christ is not attached to the form of divinity and hence is open to the form of the human. It is for this formlessness which is open to all forms that Christ is glorified. The Christian is saved by realizing the "mind of Christ." This salvation is being formless-in-form. Having the mind of Christ, the Christian is unbound by any particular form, free from any particular title and thus free for any form and title. Thus the follower of Christ is not even bound to be a follower of Christ or a carrier of the title of Christian. Nor is he afraid to be a follower of Christ or to carry the title of Christian. The Christian is completely empty and hence completely free, that is, the Christian has realized the True-Self which itself is the Christ-Self.

Karl Rahner also speaks of Christian freedom in terms of self-realization.[20] The ground of freedom, according to Rahner, is mystery. This mystery is such that the human is not defined by any category, comprehended by any idea or any system.[21] Nor is a person necessarily determined to affirm himself as this mystery. A human being can accept or reject the very ground in which he realizes Self.[22] Thus the freedom of the Christian is a freedom in which the Christian is open to all possible definitions of the "I" and constrained by none. In Zen terms, the freedom of the Christian is non-attachment to any form and hence open to the possiblity of any form. In Rahner's terms, this freedom is the freedom of freedom, a liberating of freedom from the limitations of freedom of choice and the isolation of merely inner freedom. In theological terms this liberating freedom of the human is God, a God who is mystery and yet who communicates himself to the human as grace. The surrender of the human, the openness of the human to the boundlessness which God is, is precisely the realization by the human of Self. Thus Rahner writes: "Freedom is always self-realization of the objectively choosing man seen in view of his total realization before God." [23] This realization is such that the person is purely subject and cannot be turned into an object, is purely formless (in the Zen sense) and cannot be turned into any definitive form, not even the

object that is the "not-being-an-object" or the form that is
the "not-being-a-form." Thus the freedom of the Christian
is such that he is bound into the forms of the world and yet
not constrained by these forms. It is because of this that the
freedom of the Christian is such that it can deny itself and
that the salvation of the Christian is such that it is the very
possibility for salvation or damnation.

Thus Christian freedom is the realization by each human
being of his full heritage. It is the capacity for wholeness, an
emptying of all definitions of self so that the human is open
to any definition. Freedom has as its orgin and end the God
who is mystery, a mystery which is not simply a not-know-
ing but a mystery which is a radical openness to all in
knowledge and love. This freedom is a trusting venture, an
act of faith. It is a person's dignity and task and burden.[24]
The freedom of the Christian is, finally a freedom which is
realized in the world, in the condition of finiteness, in the
situation of the human in which death is a necessity.
Salvation which is freedom cannot be realized in any other
place. Thus the human person is free in the world by not
being of the world. This freedom is established in the world
in the act of God freely present in Christ in the world.
Rahner writes:

> In so far as he became present in the world by his birth as
> the presence of God himself and remained the Son of God in
> death and made this even more tangible in his resurrection,
> Christ is the real and, indeed, tangible and visible fact of the
> free opening out of the world into God.[25]

The Christian participates in this freedom, in fact is free or
is "saved" by "having that mind in him which is in Christ
Jesus." This is not a position of inferiority or superiority. In
fact it is not a position at all but the possibility of entering
into any position. It is the human possibility of being
sensitive, of hearing deeply with compassion, of feeling

fiercely with the possibility of actively responding when active response is called for and of standing still or doing nothing when that is demanded.

Christian freedom and Zen freedom is human freedom. It is not bound by the adjectives Christian or Zen or even human. It is also not afraid to be compassionately and adamantly Christian or Zen or human. The young man hanging from the vine and exclaiming: "How tasty!" when he ate the strawberry could be a Christian or a Zen Buddhist. What he is, in the end, is himself, a self which is unattached to his condition, yet who can also be passionately concerned about that very condition. He is free.

Notes

1. Karl Rahner, *Theological Investigations*, vol. 2 (New York: Seabury, 1974), p. 92.

2. Shin-ichi Hisamatsu, "The Characteristics of Oriental Nothingness," *Philosophical Studies of Japan* 2 (1960), pp. 91–92.

3. Shin-ichi Hisamatsu, "Zen: Its Meaning for Modern Civilization," *The Eastern Buddhist*, 1-new series (1965), p. 29; D. T. Suzuki, *Essays in Zen Buddhism* (New York: Grove Press, 1949), p. 139 and *passim* throughout the writings of Suzuki; Richard DeMartino, "The Human Situation and Zen Buddhism," in *Zen Buddhism and Psychoanalysis*, D. T. Suzuki, Erich Fromm, and Richard DeMartino, eds. (New York: Grove Press, 1960), p. 154; Richard DeMartino, *The Zen Understanding of Man*, an unpublished dissertation presented at Temple University, 1969, pp. 26ff.

4. Hisamatsu as quoted by DeMartino, *The Zen Understanding of Man*, p. 39.

5. *Ibid.*, p. 41.

6. *Ibid.*, p. 41.

7. Rahner, *art. cit.*, p. 93.

8. Hui Neng as quoted by DeMartino, *The Zen Understanding of Man*, p. 34.

9. Karl Rahner, *Theological Investigations*, vol. 4, trans. by Karl-H. and Boniface Kruger (New York: Seabury, 1974), p. 194.

10. Karl Rahner, *Theological Investigations*, vol. 7, trans. by David Bourke (New York: Herder and Herder, 1971), p. 35. See also Karl Rahner, *Grace in Freedom* (New York: Herder and Herder, 1969), pp. 248–249.

11. Rahner, *Grace in Freedom*, p. 220.

12. Shin-ichi Hisamatsu, *Zen and the Fine Arts*, trans. Gishin Tokiwa (Palo Alto: Kodansha, 1971), p. 58.

13. DeMartino, *The Zen Understanding of Man*, pp. 45–46.

14. Hisamatsu, "Zen: Its Meaning for Modern Civilization," p. 30.

15. D. T. Suzuki, *Zen and Japanese Culture* (Princeton: Princeton University Press, 1959), p. 5.

16. Hisamatsu, "The Characteristics of Oriental Nothingness," pp. 93, 94.

17. Thomas Merton, *Zen and the Birds of Appetite* (New York: New Directions, 1968), pp. 10, 12.

18. *Ibid.*, p. 74.

19. Phil. 2:5.

20. Rahner, *Theological Investigations*, vol. 6, p. 193.

21. *Ibid.*, pp. 202–3.

22. *Ibid.*, p. 181.

23. *Ibid.*, p. 187.

24. *Ibid.*, p. 195.

25. Rahner, *Theological Investigations*, vol. 2, p. 96.

III THE QUESTION OF VIOLENCE

Nonviolence—A Christian Absolute?

STEPHEN J. CASEY

At a point when the focus of theological discourse is swinging from an interest in nonviolent social change to armed revolution, I think it valuable to reflect on the ethics of revolution. The initial focus for these reflections will be *The Non-Violent Cross* by James Douglass, one of the most systematic and articulate proponents of nonviolent politics to have appeared in Catholic circles. I propose neither to criticize nor defend Douglass' work, but rather to take his basic contribution to the theology of social change back to the level of its presuppositions. In the light of a radical discussion of the nature of violence, power and politics, this paper will show that there is a complex interaction of elements that precludes adherence to an absolute nonviolent ethic. At the same time it shall reject the contention that the situation is such that nonviolence must be rejected out of hand as utopian.

The Fusion of Agape and Nonviolence

The crux of Douglass' theology is found in the Christ of the gospels. While he draws insights from Gandhi, Bhave and Dolci, Douglass' ultimate commitment is to Christ as seen in the theological anthropology of Karl Rahner. From this Christocentric position, Douglass attacks the accommodations that the Church has made with the state since Constantine and the natural law rationalizations of violence that accompanied this. It is his contention that "Christ never envisioned there being 'Christian rulers' except in the form of the Satanic temptations which He rejected and overcame." [1] The post-Augustinian Church assumed moral responsibility for the state which "would always act as if it recognized no authority in Christ," [2] in the hopes that the Church could limit the violence of secular power. But Douglass argues, it was the Church that was limited. The Church compromised its catholicity by allowing an involvement with the state which made Christ and Caesar interchangeable commitments. But since Church and State recognize different ultimate authorities, we must have no delusions about the state living in Christ; the gospel had none. Further we must recognize that there will be no transformation of the world that will eliminate the tension between the ethic lived by Christ's followers and the world at large. The Church must see itself as living in diaspora; it will neither be triumphant by converting and dominating the world nor sectarian by withdrawal. Rather it must remain living in the center of that world, confronting it. The natural law base of the post-Constantinian Church must either be rejected for a Christocentric ethic or, more properly, it must be made to meet the ethical possibilities created by the grace and teachings of Christ.

The Church, says Douglass, must realize that anthropology and Christology have converged. Thus, although nonviolence is an imperative of reason and humanly demanded especially in this age, it is part of man's dependence upon God in that it can be fulfilled only in grace. It is humanly demanded because it is Christianly demanded. Contrary to the sectarian pacifists, Douglass sees "resistance to injustice . . . as much an imperative of human nature as nonviolent love is. The two values behind man are love and truth. Love means suffering and nonviolence. Truth means resistance and revolution." [3]

The theme of suffering is ever present; Douglass tells us war can bear the weight of love. Everyone, even the warrior, suffers in a war and hence can be redeemed.[4] It is sin which blocks the normal realization of the nonviolent imperative making it necessary for a redemptive love to achieve the communion of reconciliation through the incarnation of suffering.

Douglass' adherence to the nonviolent imperative is absolute. He will admit no ethical justification for bearing the sword because the only valid ethic is the gospel ethic. Natural law theorists, such as Paul Ramsay, who see war as a necessary component of justice mistakenly identify effective political power with violence.[5] Such an identification flies in the face of a pragmatic assessment of man's situation and an ethical view of his nature. Douglass maintains that in the current situation recourse to violent power-politics is likely to result in the annihilation of man by the very technology he ironically summons in his defense. At a deeper level, however, Douglass views violence as an action contrary to the nature of man; it violates man in his being. Violence is characterized by its inherent tendency toward complete destruction.

Drawing on the theories of Max Weber, Douglass argues for the acceptance of an ethic of ultimate ends. The Sermon on the Mount is one such unconditional and absolute ethic. "The Christian does rightly and leaves the results to the Lord," says Weber.[6] The primary concern of such an ethic is doing the right thing; consequences are not to be considered as decisive. To adopt this position, one must consider it in depth. Douglass uses Gandhi's insight that means are ends in process to clarify this point. To suggest that a man of faith would sin in his actions was scandalous to Gandhi; he sought redemption from sin (evil means) and not merely from the consequences of sin (an evil end). As he desired to reach the point where he did not even think of sin, he rejected the Niebuhrian position of justification by faith. He sought redemption, of course, not merely for himself but for all beings. His purpose was to bring humanity to its fullness, not to a particular goal. As the means must be present, at all times, in such a goal, Gandhi would not compromise principles. In this setting, Douglass argues, a work of "love" that destroys, even if only those things opposed to love, is mere theological abstraction. Existentially, such "love" is indistinguishable from hate and naturally arouses a counter-hatred and violence.[7]

Douglass observes that Weber's concept of politics is inapplicable to the Gandhian perspective as Weber thought in terms of rule while Gandhi thought of protest. To Weber the state is the focus of politics since the state is that "community which successfully claims the *monopoly of the legitimate use of physical force* in a given territory." Basically the state is a compulsory organization whose end is domination.[8] Gandhi believed in a nonviolent state but never fell into the utopian trap of drawing a detailed map of that distant possibility. Clearly a state can not be free of coercion (for that goes beyond its definition) but it can be nonviolent inasmuch as it is a concrete expession of the moral level of its people. Gandhi was more interested in the spiritual transformation of his people than he was in the creation of structures. As a result he worked to produce a politically intelligent citizenry that was disciplined in service, equality and sacrifice. Drawing on the civil rights struggles in the United States, Douglass adds a dimension to the Gandhian politics of protest. A politics of protest must build an independent power base if control of the established order means acceptance of corruption. The coming of the nonviolent revolution must be the result of an alternative system, the only means to preserve an alternative to violence.[9]

Defining Violence

With a pristine simplicity, Douglass describes violence as:

> ". . . an action contrary to the nature of man . . . which violates him in his being, that unique union of spirit and matter. In his whole person, man as man, demands a response of reason and respect, cooperation and friendship, love and communion. Violence . . . [has] an inherent tendency toward complete destruction.[10]

Douglass resembles other theoreticians in several instances:[11] in his insistence on the primacy of human integrity and rights, his specification of violence as the infringement or suspension of that integrity, and his refusal to restrict violence to physical force or attack. Although some social scientists argue for a narrow definition of violence,[12] limiting violence to the extreme end of the spectrum of aggressive behavior, Douglass insists on this broader concept. He argues that a narrow definition deceives society about causes of violence by failing to place the covert exploitation of established power blocks on the same plane as the openly violent reaction that springs from such exploitation.[13]

Yet Douglass' definition can also be amplified. Newton Garver bids us break down violence into the categories of individual and collective, covert and overt. We quickly see that war (collective and overt violence) and muggings (individual and covert violence) are a small part of violence. Paternalism (social and individual but covert) merges with economic exploitation (also covert) as assaults on the autonomy of persons. Each restricts man's freedom to make decisions and to exercise his subsidiary right to receive the benefits of those decisions. The covert violence, regardless of the context, is most difficult to resist. Because there is less physical manifestation of such violence, it is more difficult to identify the perpetrator or to resist him. Covert violence takes the ground out from under its victim because a victimizer may argue that no violence is actually being done. The usual contention is that routine social patterns are the cause of the injury, hence no violence is present; many observers will agree.[14]

A full treatment of violence must include a discussion of threat which can be the bridge between covert and overt violence. Threatening promises the physical enactment of a hidden encroachment either with physical or psychological violence. The threat may involve a covert action such as undermining a person's social or economic standing, thereby doing him or her harm. It suggests harm in order to coerce, i.e., to cause a person to act without autonomy or free consent. Such action fits within Douglass' and Garver's definitions. However, in considering the threat we are obliged to go beyond a definition of violence to a fuller exploration of the nature of politics, for the question of the threat and coercion in a social context raises anew the issue of political interaction.

Any discussion of the state and politics seems to evolve to the point where theoreticians, left and right, suggest that violence is the ultimate power and the state is the ultimate organizer of that violence. This contention is based on the view, like Marx's, that government is and must be a form of exploitation. The use of violence in the name of law and order is a mask for preserving control by governmental powers. While the Marxist presupposition is not without merit, I think it desirable to explore another perhaps parallel source of power.

Hannah Arendt in her work on violence suggests that the confusion about politics and the state arises from confusing force with power.[15] She contends that the deliberate restriction of force can change its quality. The classical political theorists decided that power rests not on a command-obedience base (that is an identification of power and rule) but on a consent base. The rule of law, the restraint imposed on government in a democracy, is the result of the citizenry's consent to support those laws. The power of such a state rests upon numbers; its power increases with the number consenting and decreases with the number dissenting. This power flows, then, from the ability of a group to act in concert. No one can argue, especially in a post-Watergate era, that there is always consent and concert in such arrangements. It is possible to short-circuit such a consent arrangement by the application of violent force—overt and covert. Such actions circumscribe or contrain human freedom. One is quickly tempted, however, to suggest that Arendt's concept is idealistic or utopian and violence is the *de facto* condition of politics. In fact, there is a middle ground that must be explored.

H. L. Nieburg in his work *Political Violence*[16] suggests that our society is marked by two outstanding political facts: social change is endemic, and groups compete in a continual bargaining process to maintain their standing in the shifting political sands. The actions of these groups range from polite suggestions on a golf course to a violent riot or insurrection. The means employed in such a bargaining process are determined by such things as the access of the parties to the media and persons in authority, by the relative strength and discipline of the group, and by the framework in which the bargaining takes place. The political process so conceived is closely tied to the process of socialization and, significantly, is also tied to the establishment of a moral code. Human behavior is based on experience, on trial and error, on bargaining. In some ways our value systems are adjusted to be consistent with our behavior. Thus, integration forced upon the average citizen by open housing laws is accepted and rationalized. At the same time a citizen can, while preserving his self-pride, become a believer in equal rights in housing. Such a change in attitude will not occur if several factors are not present.[17]

Persons involved must have at least some sympathy for the general ideals reflected in the law, their actions must have consequences and they must be personally responsible for acting. As a general statement, we can say that real decision-making and bargaining modifies behavior, attitudes and relationships. Nieburg contends that principles and ideologies are meaningless except when reinforced by a strong bargaining position, i.e., one that can result in modification of behavior. Be that as it may, it is important to see the advantages of this view of politics for our discussion.

Nieburg's bargaining concept preserves both a "realistic" position and one that is oriented toward a future less violent. Violence is part of the political process, but it is not exalted or justified in an ultimate sense. It is rather viewed as one of a variety of responses possible and hence to be expected in political conflict. By preserving the continuity between the socialization process and the political process, this view allows us to see the connection between covert, institutionalized violence and its overt *ad hoc* brother. When we understand that consent brings concerted action and hence power to a group, we can see how threats, especially covert ones, may have much use in politics. Finally, we can see that politics need not make distinctions between rule and protest, as they, too, are part of a single spectrum. When one does not have power by consent, one must resort to physical force, i.e., a concept of power as the right to demand obedience. It must further be observed that the bargaining-consent model resembles more adequately the actual framework and dynamic of government today. Revolution occurs in a situation where those in power employ the police and armed forces to maintain the status quo without a genuine bargaining relationship with the majority of citizens. The system of government will then undergo an abrupt alteration in an attempt to be more representative of actual power. Finally, this model is fluid.

In this way, it admits rapid social change that could be affected by nonviolent power without vast destruction, at least some of the time.

It appears therefore that Nieburg's understanding of the relationship between politics, power and violence enables us to transcend the polarizing simplicity of Douglass' absolute insistence upon nonviolence. In adopting Weber's projection of an ideal type of society and translating it into a vision of required Christian procedure, Douglas falsely envisions as absolute a value that must unfortunately remain relative in a still sinful world.

The Necessary Ambivalence of Violence

A Christian must enter the political arena, for abstention means abdication of responsibility. To remain outside of politics is to consent to present evils and to deny the possibility of redemption for this realm of life. At the same time, any Christian inclined to enter the political arena ought to heed the words of Max Weber, "The final results of political action often, no, even regularly, stand in completely inadequate and often paradoxical relation to their original meaning." [18] Yet if, with Hannah Arendt, we see the generalized type of violence that we have discussed as "instrumental," we will be able to comprehend its moral qualities as well as its ambivalence.[19] To suggest that violence is instrumental is to suggest that it stands in need of guidance and ultimate justification. As an instrument, violence *must* be ambivalent to the Christian. As Arendt points out, the ends of human action can never be reliably predicted as can the ends of human fabrication.[20] Such ambivalence is reflected in Karl Rahner's treatise on power.[21] His first premise is that the power that uses physical means, a power that is not addressed to freedom and insight, should not exist. His second premise is that this power is a gift of God and it is not sinful to use it. The key to this understanding is in Rahner's explanation of sin and power. Man is not able to integrate fully the reality of his existence into those decisions that affect his freedom. The result is a dichotomy between what man is and wants to be. Man must face powers that are contrary to his freedom continually. Power is not sin but rather a manifestation of sin. As man is a material and interpersonal being, he is tied to concrete expressions of self. When he expresses his freedom, he does so in a common sphere of existence where, of necessity, he ends up restricting another's space for freedom. This power becomes a form of coercion and hence violence. Because a material sphere is a necessary prerequisite of freedom Rahner declares that power and freedom exist in a dialectical interdependence.[22] It is true that freedom is of a higher order as it is of the spirit, but power, while it is lower and a limitation of the spirit, is necessary. Rahner declares that the *absolute* renunciation of force, i.e., the renunciation of the exercise of freedom in a material order, is immoral. But politics is necessarily of that material order. To suggest that power is a gift of God and necessary (hence not sinful) is not to suggest that power is a static entity. It will always remain dangerous. The exercise of a freedom that becomes "a barrier to the sin of another can . . . become the concrete form of (one's) own sinfulness." [23] If this is the case, one must agree with Arendt that "the means employed to achieve political goals are, more often than not, of greater relevance to the future than the intended goals." [24]

Clearly this view of politics must lead to a rejection of the Weberian ethical model which separates political responsibility and the ethics of the gospel. Gene Sharp observes that Weber makes several time-bound assumptions in his framework.[25] He assumes that to be responsible one must be ready to use essentially evil means in politics. Such an assumption flows from an easy acceptance of the conventional political wisdom of his day. It was thought that nonviolence, the means Weber associated with the ethics of ultimate ends, could not be politically effective and thus could not be politically responsible. Such a position is untenable.[26] Sharp notes that little consensus has been reached on the long range consequences of nonviolence. Thus, while he is anxious to reformulate Weber's models of ethics, he does not intend to do it in terms of responsibility or maturity.[27] Instead Sharp has replaced Weber's design with a five part model based upon various understandings of the inter-relationship between means and ends. Put brieflly, his categories are:

1. Ethics of loyalty to ultimate ends—without concern for the results.
2. Ethics of deliberate consistency in means and ends.
3. Ethics of willingness to use the "necessary" and "most suitable" means.
4. Ethics of "necessary evil" of violence.
5. Ethics of loyalty to violence.[28]

Numbers one, three, four and five can be rejected as valid models, especially in light of our previous considerations. One is merely Weber's category of ultimate ends. Four and five deny the efficacy of any political means except violence. The reasons for the rejection of number three are more complex. This position is primarily concerned with immediate political effectiveness and only secondarily with principles and long-range goals. Little attention will be paid to a connection between means and ends if this model is used over a period of time. Violence is efficacious—too efficacious. In the short run, it provides the most effective and, hence, attractive means to reach a material goal. One can easily become enamored of it and lose sight of long range goals and consequences. The employment of such a model would cause one to lose sight of means other than violence and thereafter make no attempt to restrain violence. What is needed is a model employing means which point toward an end beyond the immediate conflict, regarded as a manifestation of the lack of mastery of man's self that Rahner noted. Sharp's second model seems to do this. The adherent of this model will organize to produce desired social-political ends on the assumption that the means must contain some element of the end. Such a person would work with others not commited to a principled nonviolence but who are willing to apply nonviolent measures to particular problems. This position provides a model that can readily be adapted to the framework of politics we have laid. Two additions, however, must be made before we can see this approach as a useful focal point in our discussion.

The first is that the nonviolence we have discussed is principled, i.e., motivated by a force outside of itself. As Miller observed there is a difference between the self-expending love of the gospel and nonviolence.[29] The source of direction and the ultimate justification for nonviolence is found by the Christian in agape. Nonviolence becomes a principle because of agape. It must be noted, however, that violence and nonviolence are not on an equal footing. "Power is something to be gradually modified and absorbed by love like concupiscence."[30] This brings us to our second point.

While our discussion revolves around principled nonviolence, this essay has attempted to show that such a principle is not absolute. Some violence, at least in the form of coercion, seems inevitable. I have chosen to opt for a view of nonviolence as a force coming into being. While Sharp does not include such an element in his model, I think that it is necessary.

Eschatological Tension Between Politics and Nonviolence

The tension between what man is and what he wants to be is the same as the tension between principled nonviolence and its introduction into the political arena. Today we argue that absolute nonviolence is chimerical; we advocate action in politics that may include coercion, arguing that it is relatively more acceptable because it allows redemptive modification while structured overt violence precludes this. This cannot always be so. As Rahner noted, we act to remove the sources of evil within ourselves; and these are not always the same. However, we do not expect evil to disappear although we do expect it to disappear with the coming of the escaton. Today, as never before, eschatology is an element in our consideration of the present and it can provide us with insight into the application of the principles of nonviolence.

In the late thirties, several writers on biblical matters set the stage for our present ideas. They observed a problem that is well stated by W. G. Kümmel in his *Promise And Fulfillment*: "What meaning is there in the fact that Jesus placed side by side the conceptions that the Kingdom of God was expected soon, that its coming was expected within his generation, and that the Kingdom of God was present; in addition to this he even emphasized that the hour of its coming is unknown?" [31] If one takes the eschatological statements of the gospel seriously, Kümmel's question leads one to an interesting view of history and salvation. Thus C. H. Dodd points out, "While the New Testament affirms with full seriousness that the great divine event has occurred, there remains a residue of eschatology which is not exhausted in the 'realized' eschatology of the gospel, namely, the element of sheer finality." [32] There is, then, a two-level eschatology that has immediate consequences for our concept of redemption. The eschatological event ushering in the new era has occurred: Jesus was present as man, has suffered, died and risen. Yet there will be a second coming. The Kingdom of God is not yet present in its finality. In terms of nonviolence, the message of eschatology may be this. In the eschatological event of Jesus and his suffering, death and resurrection, we see the action of God in history. However, the action is not fully understood as we are in a process of moving toward its fullness. We cannot ignore the commitment to the way of God; we must try to begin a nonviolent life. At the same time we cannot hope either to achieve perfection or to see our way fully to that perfection so we can freely embrace it.[33]

This tentative nature of the truth of nonviolence is evident in John Dunne's *The Way of All The Earth*.[34] Dunne distinguishes between the possession of truth and the "enforcement" of truth. He retells one of Lessing's tales about God: if God held truth in his right hand and the life-long pursuit of it in his left, Lessing would choose the left. Man has received various revelations of what God is doing, but in spite of everything the revelations have not brought man to completion. God holds out to man the offer of the life-long pursuit of truth, and it seems that man cannot jump stages of development to the end. He must plumb the depth of the scriptures until his actions become like the actions of God.[35] Yet he must admit that that God is in disguise and can be known only by "passing over" in an experiment with truth. Passing over involves a shifting of viewpoint to another way of life, culture or religion. It is accompanied by an equal and opposite process of coming back, i.e., returning with insight to one's own way of life, culture or religion. The figure most closely associated with this process is Gandhi. He called his odyssey an "experiment with truth," meaning that he sought to achieve the ultimate truth by various attempts to enforce truth in actual life situations. Making concrete the poetry of revelation in life should enable man to see the basic limitations of the human condition. Dunne suggests that man will never come to a knowledge of what he is doing until he comes to a knowledge of what God is doing. An understanding of what God is doing then will give us insight into the nature of nonviolence.

The God revealed to us in our odyssey is one who cares for each and every being in the midst of time. This God is not merely present at the genesis and the final end of creation, He is in the midst of time coming among men. As Dunne points out, man often tries to escape creation to find God. He likens this trip to a climb up a mountain. When man reaches the pinnacle, he finds that God has passed him on his trip to the valley below. One finds God not in the solitude of the mountain but in the conflict of the valley.

Dunne also points out that a key characteristic of God's presence for man is that he has renounced the fruits of His action, i.e., He involves himself in human history without any isolated, merely personal goals to achieve. A God who acts in this manner must be concerned very much with the action and not with the consequences. This God cares, but he cares in terms of creative action. His labors are for man and He wishes man to see this process and share in it.

For man to understand this requires a drastic change of viewpoint. When anyone acts hoping to benefit from their actions, they become ensnarled in a web of cross purposes. As Gandhi recognized from his reading of the Gita, one can escape this web only by renouncing the fruits of his action. But if man begins to act in this way, to act as God does, he will begin a process of discovery that is pervaded by a knowledge of his own ignorance. This pursuit of knowledge is not the possession of it, but rather the start of a progressive unfolding. The implications of this for political action and nonviolence are many.

One must begin to practice nonviolence in the valley of politics for it is a manifestation of the action of God in history. One must do it, however, with the knowledge that man is on a journey of creation with God in time. Man must recognize that nonviolence must begin in a concrete situation and then transform it. This is an "experiment with truth" that will determine the limits of the human condition. In the change that will take place, man must leave certain elements behind: thoughts of victory and control, as well as the violence of exploitation. "Power will be used not *because* I have it but *although* I have it." [36] One acts, after all, only for the good of others if one has renounced the fruits of action. But this stress on creative action is a liberating one. Concern over immediate results produces anxiety, and with it an attempt to achieve certainty through rigid formulae of conduct. Stress on the action offers a vision of the boundlessness of God and a creation which mirrors him. Such a vision places escatology in context and provides a context in which we can begin the understanding of nonviolence.

Notes

1. James Douglass, *The Non-Violent Cross* (New York: Macmillan, 1968), p. 207.
2. *Ibid.*, p. 208.
3. *Ibid.*, p. 234.
4. *Ibid.*, p. 239.
5. *Ibid.*, p. 174.
6. Max Weber, *Politics As A Vocation*, trans. H. H. Gerth and C. Wright Mills (Philadelphia: Fortress Press, 1965), pp. 45–7.
7. Douglass, *op. cit.*, p. 249.
8. Weber, *op. cit.*, pp. 2–7.
9. Douglass, *op. cit.*, pp. 266–9.
10. *Ibid.*, p. 220.
11. See, for instance, William Miller, *Non-Violence* (New York: Schocken, 1964); Newton Garver, "What Violence Is", *Violence in America*, ed. Thomas Rose (New York: Random House, 1969); Robert Audi, "On the Meaning and Justification of Violence," *Violence*, ed. Jerome Shaffer (New York: David McKay, 1971).
12. See, for instance, John Spiegel, *Transactions*, ed. John Papajohn (New York: Science House, 1971), pp. 339–354. Ronald B. Miller, "Violence, Force and Coercion," *Violence*, ed. Jerome Shaffer (New York: David McKay, 1971).
13. See also H. D. Graham and T. R. Gurr, *Violence in America* (New York: Bantam, 1969).

14. Spiegel, *op. cit.*

15. Hannah Arendt, *On Violence* (New York: Harcourt, Brace and World, 1970), p. 37ff. These ideas are essentially hers. Two other commentators in essential agreement are J. C. Murray, *We Hold These Truths* (New York: Sheed and Ward, 1960) and Gene Sharp, *The Politics of Non-Violent Action* (Boston: Porter Sargent, 1973).

16. H. L. Nieburg, *Political Violence* (New York: St. Martin's, 1969). The following discussion is drawn from his concepts.

17. See Michael Hoyt, "Personal Responsibility for Consequences: An Integration and Extension of 'Forced Compliance' Literature," *Journal of Experimental Social Psychology* 8 (1972), pp. 558–593. See also: Gordon W. Allport, *The Nature of Prejudice* (Garden City: Doubleday, 1954).

18. Weber, *op. cit.*, p. 43.

19. Arendt, *op. cit.*, p. 51.

20. *Ibid.*, p. 3.

21. Karl Rahner, "The Theology of Power" in *Theological Investigations IV*, trans. Kevin Smyth (New York: Seabury, 1974).

22. *Ibid.*, p. 399.

23. *Ibid.*, p. 395.

24. Arendt, *op. cit.*, p. 3.

25. Gene Sharp, "Ethics and Responsibility in Politics," *Inquiry* (Oslo) 3 (1964), p. 306.

26. One need only review Sharp's *magnum opus, The Politics of Non-Violent Action*, to see numerous cases disproving this. The same is true of cases in Miller's *Non-Violence* and A. Paul Hare-Herbert Blumberg, eds. *Non-Violent Direct Action* (Washington: Corpus, 1968). One can open the paper to read about the general strike in Northern Ireland if a current case is important.

27. One may also note that the question of definition is a more serious antecedent problem. When we are attempting to define violence (or nonviolence), crime or delinquency, we are engaging in a political action. The labeling has a direct effect upon the relationships and bargaining positions of various groups (see Nieburg, p. 65ff). Many white Americans consider burning a draft card violent (59%) but don't agree that the shooting of looters by police is violent (only 39% thought so). These figures do not apply to Blacks; 59% thought that the shooting of looters was

violent and 51% believed that burning draft cards was violent. (See Robert Kahn's "Who Buys Bloodshed and Why?" in *Psychology Today*, June 1972, p. 47ff). The question of an ascribed reputation is raised in "Who Defines Delinquency?" by Leroy Gould (*Social Problems*, 16 [1969], p. 325–336). Gould reports on an interview done with youths officially labeled "delinquent." The group included Whites, Blacks and Orientals. Using a standardized form, he asked them to describe their previous actions and themselves. Only the Whites described themselves in the same manner as the official reports did. Blacks and Orientals did not consider themselves delinquent.

28. Sharp, "Ethics and Responsibility in Politics", pp. 314–315.

29. Miller, *op. cit.*, p. 23f.

30. Rahner, *art. cit.*, p. 406.

31. W. G. Kümmel, *Promise and Fulfillment*, trans. D. M. Barton (London: S. C. M. Press, 1957), p. 141.

32. C. H. Dodd, *The Apostolic Preaching* (New York: Harper Brothers, 1936), p. 93.

33. When dealing with eschatology, it is important to note the work of Jürgen Moltmann. Moltmann is, however, decidedly unconcerned with nonviolence: "The problem of violence and nonviolence is an illusory one. There is only a question of the justified and unjustified use of force and the question of whether the means are proportionate." *Religion, Revolution and the Future*, trans. by M. D. Meeks (New York: Scribner's, 1969), p. 143f.

34. John Dunne, *The Way of All the Earth* (New York: Macmillan, 1972).

35. *Ibid.*, Part I, chapter iii, section 4.

36. Rahner, *art. cit.*, p. 407.

The Psychological Origins of Violence and Revolution

LEONARD J. BIALLAS

One dimension often sidetracked in various theologies of liberation is the nature and alleviation of violence. To be sure, there is usually a consideration of the arguments for and against Jesus as revolutionary or as suffering servant, the arguments for and against violence and nonviolence, and perhaps even a vague statement on revolutionary violence being justified and necessary to combat an evil political system. The roots and cures of violence and aggression, however, are generally passed by. Happily many psychologists have considered this very dimension in the past several years, especially in the wake of the two World Wars and the student riots and black riots of the 1960's.[1] While vigorously rejecting the notion that psychologists can fully explain violence and conflict, theology can fruitfully investigate their discussions.

The Classical Theories

The two main theories on the sources and prescriptions for violence have been characterized variously as "nature vs. nurture," instinct vs. learning, or inborn violence vs. violence as a result of experience. More recently psychologists seem to say that these two classical positions are not mutually exclusive: aggression and violence are not only instinctual drives rooted in the human condition, but are also culturally formed and controlled. This is expressed by Carl Gustav Jung and Rollo May. Before considering their position, we will look at the two classical theories.

Two key men who hold that violence or aggression (physical behavior with the intent to injure or destroy) is *innate* are Sigmund Freud and Konrad Lorenz.[2] In Freud's view, man possesses two opposing instincts: life (eros) which causes the person to grow and survive, and death (thanatos) which works toward the individual's self-destruction. Often this death instinct is redirected and becomes aggression against others. When there are no socially acceptable outlets for this death-energy, it will accumulate and eventually be released in some extreme violence. Lorenz studied animal behavior and concluded that man's aggression as manifested in war, crime and other kinds of destructive behavior is due to a genetically programmed, innate instinct which waits for the proper occasion to be discharged. The best man can do is understand the law of evolution that accounts for the power of this drive. Neither Freud nor Lorenz are concerned that a person's violent actions, unlike an animal's, are often in response to memories and ideas rather than immediate situations, and are often carried out without ever coming into contact with the victim.

For the control of violence, the proponents of the "nature" theory suggest various solutions.[3] 1) A deeper insight is required into the laws of evolution. Knowledge of the role of the unconscious, of emotions, and of intentionality is not considered important. 2) Promotion of personal acquaintances and genuine friendship between individual members of different ideologies or nations is desirable. This approach, however, disregards the fact that this intimacy often increases hatred, and that civil wars are often the worst of all wars. 3) Since outbreaks of international violence are often connected with population increases and the consequent need for economic/territorial expansion, the "nature" theory of violence urges greater efforts toward birth control and the acceptance of euthanasia. Yet it would seem that violence is merely a symptom of the disease which is powerlessness or injustice. Fewer people does not necessarily mean less violence. 4) Energy and enthusiasm should be channeled into socially acceptable outlets such as athletic competition. But such outlets often further competitive aggressiveness and nationalistic pride.

The other classical position—that violence is socially *learned* or due to response to frustrations, rewards, and punishments—is taken by John Dollard and Neal Miller, and B. F. Skinner.[4] Dollard and Miller formulate a frustration-aggression theory, which has been modified by several people; they state that every frustration produces an instigation of aggression. Frustration here is understood either as the imposed interruption of an on-going, goal-directed activity, or the negation of some desire or wish. Thus Dollard and Miller are not concerned with subjective forces or feelings, but with external behavior and social conditioning. For Skinner, too, the deed, not the doer, is the object for scientific investigation. A person persists only in that behavior which is rewarding to himself. If his conditioning is adequate, then he will be well-adjusted; if not, then society must suffer for his aggressiveness and violence. If the person is deprived of love from infancy, or grows up with the continual experience of conflict, then helplessness and disregard may force him to avoid close relationships and be depressed or aggressive.

Proponents of the nurture theory also suggest various solutions for the alleviation of violence. 1) Control the awareness of violence by limiting its place in television and the news media. 2) Encourage methods of education for children where frustration is diminished. 3) Suppress violent behavior which is otherwise uncontrollable by isolating the violent members of a society. 4) Displace or regulate violence through identification with nonviolent heroes.

This position also raises several problems. Violent or aggressive reactions can occur without prior frustration. For example, children tend to imitate adult behavior, even if it is aggressive. Also many times frustration does not produce aggression. Thirdly, motivation or anonymity can change behavior—a father may spank a child out of love or out of sadism, and a member of the Ku Klux Klan may be more boldly aggressive with his hood on. And finally, this approach dehumanizes us, considering us as animals that can be programmed to do anything.

Jung's Approach to Violence

The criticisms and problems inherent in these two classical positions should incline the theologian to consider those psychologists who hold a third position—that violence is both a part of the human condition and culturally formed and controlled. Here I would like to consider Jung and May.[5] For them the intellect alone is not sufficient: the entire psyche is responsible for one's growth and self-affirmation. For them the unconscious is a reality that is experienced and permeates a person on all levels: feeling, acting, thinking, and deciding. In their psychoanalysis they add a depth-dimension to reality, one that is organic and purposive, one that incorporates the past and anticipates the future. Jung and May disagree somewhat, though, in their conclusions about violence. Jung feels that violence is due to one's lack of awareness of the unconscious, and the cure is to "heal oneself" through the process of individuation, while May holds that violence is a symptom of powerlessness, and the solution is power tempered by love or compassion.

Basic to Jung's understanding of the origin of violence is

the fundamental axiom that every psychic phenomenon is compensated for by its opposite. He illustrates this, for example, by commenting on the two contrary principles, the bright yang and the dark yin in classical Chinese philosophy. When one principle is reaching the height of its power, the counter-principle is stirring within it like a seed. Jung also explains violence in terms of the alchemical symbol, the *uroboros,* the snake that devours itself and brings itself to life: from its own death, it rises again to new life. In the Christian tradition, this axiom is manifested in the opposition between God and the devil. Also, it is symbolized in Christ, the Alpha and the Omega: in Him is found the course of all things from the beginning to the end and from the end back to the beginning. These various examples all illustrate that a man's life cannot be otherwise than full of conflicts, for two forces are at war within him: on the one hand the justified longing of the ordinary man for happiness, satisfaction, and security, and on the other hand a ruthless passion for creation which may go so far as to override and destroy every personal desire.

Such insistence on the reality of opposites in all realms of life, including the psyche, is indispensable to Jung's discussion of violence. He feels that Christians especially are too quick to attribute violence and evil to the devil, the personification of evil, rather than admit the devilishness of their own nature. They foist off responsibility and guilt on spiritual forces outside themselves. In denying conflict inside themselves, they deny the possibility of ethical decisions. Thus, in the nature-nurture discussion, Jung would say that man is both good and evil by nature, but he is conditioned by his culture to believe that evil exists only outside of himself.

Evil is essential for man, according to Jung. If evil were to be utterly destroyed, human experience would be impoverished. Thus Jung denies the patristic position that evil (and *a fortiori* violence) is a privation of good, having no substance or existence in itself.[6] Jung's findings told him otherwise: psychological experience shows that whatever we call "good" is balanced by an equally substantial "bad" or "evil." Besides, what may appear to one person as good will appear to another as evil: there is a relativity of values both on a personal and a national level. To pursue the certitude of always knowing what is good and evil is to give in to the temptation of Paradise: if they ate of the tree, they would be as gods, knowing good and evil.

According to Jung, the devil, though created, is autonomous and eternal.[7] He is the adversary of Christ, and the occasion for God's incarnation in Christ. Today we give the devil a different name; we call the source of evil a neurosis. But the same experience is implied: something not under man's control fixedly opposed to the sovereignty of man's will. This is the reality that many people will not admit exists objectively in the psyche. Jung calls it the "shadow." [8] To repress this primitive, unadapted and awkward reality is to force it into revolt. It is to create another structure of death around us.

Surely it is better to acknowledge that the worst enemy is within the self. Refusal to admit this results in projecting evil onto someone else who is then considered the enemy. This is the origin of violence, for such projections inevitably arouse anger and make a person aggressive. Internal forces encroach on the consciousness and take it by surprise and violence. With a projection of evil onto others, everybody suffers—the victim and the aggressor.

Conflicts within the individual, then, are projected in the forms of political tension and murderous violence. The value and importance of the individual then rapidly decreases. The force of evil in society, the "malignity of collective man" becomes so strong that peace is unthinkable and any world order is imperilled. The individual shuns responsibility and turns to the state for a collective feeling of security. Thus he has no protection against his inner shadow and clings all the more to the power of the state, i.e., to the masses, delivering himself up to it psychically as well as morally in the effort to overcome his social impotence.[9]

May's Emphasis on Powerlessness

Rollo May accepts Jung's ideas on ignorance of the shadow and projection of this shadow onto others, and goes even further. May sees violence as a symptom of the daimonic (roughly, in Jung's terms, the shadow) gone awry, or as a sense of powerlessness in society. For May, too, daimonic figures are psychologically necessary. They have to exist to make human action and freedom possible. The hope that Satan or other adversaries can be gotten rid of by gradual progress toward perfection would not be a constructive idea even if it were possible. This unnamed, impersonal combination of good and evil is necessary for constructive growth. The daimonic becomes evil when it usurps the total self, or when it usurps the desires of others and their need for integration. It then appears as excessive aggression and hostility. With Jung, May feels that the daimonic tends to explode in violence if a person represses it. The daimonic should not be destroyed, but must be acknowledged. To rule it out is itself daimonic: it makes the person an accomplice on the side of destructive possession.[10]

In addition to its origin in the daimonic, May says that violence may arise from one's contact, or lack of contact, with others in society. Violence then is the destructive substitute which surges in to fill the vacuum where there is no relatedness between people, where there is apathy. Violence comes when one cannot genuinely touch another person. It flares up as a necessity for contact, a mad drive forcing touch in the most direct way possible. It is the predictable end result after a person is denied what he feels are his legitimate rights, after he is burdened with feelings of impotence which corrode his remaining self-esteem. It is the explosion of the drive to destroy all barriers to movement and personal growth. Violence and aggression are largely physical because other phases of power (the power to be, the power of self-affirmation, the power of self-assertion) have been blocked off: "we often speak of the tendency toward violence as building up inside the individual, but it is also a response to outside conditions. The source of violence must be seen in both its internal and external manifestations, a response to a situation which is felt to block off all other ways of response." [11]

Such an expression of powerlessness is true also in international relations. Here, however, violence comes even from the very threat of impotence: "Nations seem to find it necessary to protect themselves on a periphery farther out; they must be aware, precariously balanced as they are on the seesaw of armaments, of whether another country is building up power to gain an advantage over them. If a nation becomes genuinely impotent, it is no longer a nation." [12] This is heightened, of course, when dialogue breaks down: the daimonic is projected onto the enemy which then becomes not another nation with its own security and power needs, but the personification of the devil. People abdicate responsibility, become rigid, and make decisions not in their own best interest. The daimonic again expresses itself as a blind unconscious push, and depersonalizes people on both sides.

Liberation from Violence: Jung

Jung and May will not go along with any solution or cure for violence that does not admit that it is necessary for healthy growth. What then do they offer by way of liberation from violence? Both of them acknowledge the need of help from the transcendent, with Jung stressing the importance of the Christ-symbol who is the personification of wholeness, and May centering his reflections around Christ the rebel and the ideal of compassion.

For Jung, the individual has to realize that salvation is non-rational, that is, it always comes from outside the individual. The individual needs the Comforter, the Paraclete, because he cannot overcome the conflict with his own resources. He has to rely on divine comfort and mediation, that is, on the spontaneous revelation of the Spirit, usually manifested through dreams. If the violence projected outwards is to be controlled, the individual must realize its unconscious origin in his psyche. This is the first step in liberation. He must recognize and accept the daimonic in himself. Perhaps this is the meaning of Christ's teaching that each must bear his own cross: "Only through the most extreme and most menacing conflict does the Christian experience deliverance into divinity, always provided that he does not break, but accepts the burden of being marked out by God. In this way alone can the *imago Dei* realize itself in him, and God become man." [13] Wholeness is self-awareness. In addition to faith, hope, and love, a person needs the self-understanding which is the grace that the Paraclete brings. For Jung the apocryphal insertion at Luke 6:4 is important: "Man if thou knowest what thou doest, thou art blessed, but if thou knowest not, thou art cursed and a transgressor of the law." Negligence in understanding one's unconscious makes a person an instrument of evil, and what is worse, deprives him of his capacity to deal with evil.[14]

Recognition of evil in the self is the first step in the process of liberation, in what Jung calls healing, self-reconciliation, or individuation. When fully developed, a person is aware of the totality of his psyche, consisting of consciousness and unconsciousness, and is ready to apply the Christian virtues of forgiveness and love of one's enemies to his own person. Such a separation and deliverance from an earlier condition of darkness and unconsciousness, leads to victory and transcendence over everything "given." It is the mystic experience of "letting oneself go," leading to the new man, the completely transformed man, one who has broken the shell of the old ego and who not only looks upon a new heaven and a new earth, but has helped create them. This may be done by imitating Christ, not in blind obedience but in realizing one's deepest conviction with the same courage and self-sacrifice that Jesus showed. Happily not every one has the task of being a leader of humanity or a great rebel and so, after all, it might be possible for each to realize himself in his own way.[15]

The incarnation of God is the archetype of each person's process of individuation. Becoming human is an heroic and often tragic task, involving great suffering, even on the part of God. God became man to give man the model for suffering, for suffering is the price to pay for realizing one's wholeness.[16] The central role of Christ is precisely that in Him we have an apocatastasis, a restoring of the initial state in an eschatological one. Christ is the living myth of western culture, the hero who proves to be a mediator by offering man an approach to divinity, through conquering the demon within. Christ is God and man at the same time and therefore suffers a divine as well as a human fate. In the incarnate God is the reconciliation of opposites, the yin and yang, the uroboros, the mandala, the circle, all symbols of wholeness, healing, redemption, and liberation.[17]

Liberation from Violence: May

Rollo May, in addition to alleviating violence and evil through recognition of the daimonic, emphasizes the positive role of the rebel in channeling daimonic forces in constructive directions and the need for a fusion of power and love in compassion. Following the characterization of Camus, May distinguishes between the rebel and the revolutionary. Where the revolutionary fights for external political change and tries to amass power, the rebel breaks with established customs to share power and to keep people from settling into complacency. The rebel fights for his own personal integrity out of a vision of compassion and responsibility for others. Jesus himself was a rebel, as May describes one:

> The rebel does what the rest of us would like to do but don't dare. Note that Christ willingly takes on himself the sins and the scorn of men; he acts, lives, and dies, vicariously for the rest of us. This is what makes him a rebel. The rebel and the savior then turn out to be the same figure. Through his rebellion the rebel saves us.[18]

He challenged the structure and stability of the very society that nursed Him and gave him security to develop His potentialities (cf. Matthew 5: "It was said of old . . . but *I* say to you."). His concern was not the society as it was, but the community as it could be. Jesus as a rebel maintained the balance between Dionysius and Apollo and shared this balance with the community: the dynamic blend of joy, dancing, and release from inhibitions with a healthy, rational, and fixed stability of vision (the Kingdom).

Perhaps the rebel will have to be violent. In a society where many are powerless, violence or aggression performs the constructive function of redistributing and sharing the power for self-affirmation and self-assertion. It can be life-giving rather than life-destroying. May writes:

> If, as is our tendency in this country, we condemn all violence out of hand and try to eradicate even the possibility of violence from a human being, we take away from him an element that is essential to his full humanity. For the self-respecting human being, violence is always an ultimate possibility—and it will be resorted to less if admitted than if suppressed. For the free man it remains in imagination an ultimate exit when all other avenues are denied by unbeara-

ble tyranny or dictatorship over the spirit as well as the body.[19]

Violence performs a healing function: it cuts through barriers to initiate relationships with others; it makes a person feel that he too counts and shares responsibility for his friends; it develops unity within a people by affirming their dignity, their potential consciousness, and their future freedom.[20]

In no way is May advocating unbridled violence. What he calls for is rather the exercise of power tempered with love. Social action—working for racial justice and international peace, helping the poor—would not be possible without a combination of power and love. Love needs power if it is to be more than sentimentality; power needs love if it is not to slide into manipulation.[21] There is, however, a form of love which transcends power, and this is compassion. Compassion is the basis of May's new ethic which goes beyond any merely human Utopia by recognizing the reality of God's grace. High purpose is not enough: what is necessary is a religious commitment that transcends the members of the community and saves them from believing that changes will occur because they want them or that one can escape the tragedy and complexity of life by ignoring the presence of the daimonic.

In fact, compassion is not violence, for violence projects hostile images on the opponent, while compassion accepts such daimonic impulses in the self. Compassion recognizes that each person has a capacity for evil, and that achievement is bound up with the very conflicts that a person's daimonic impulse engenders. Compassion demands authentic empathy, an identification with the woes and joys of those who lack power. It is a recognition that life consists of achieving good not apart from evil but in spite of it. It is to admit that good and evil dwell within the same person, and that one's potentiality increases in proportion to his capacity for good.[22]

A Theological Response

The theology of liberation can certainly incorporate the "healing" function that is fulfilled by recognizing the necessity of conflict. Also, the ideals of the rebel and the idea of compassion are not without merit. However, neither Jung nor May recognize the function of the church and the centrality of the resurrection. True, they stress that morality should not be a personal endurance contest, and recognize the necessity of the spirit, but neither comments on the function of the witness and fellowship of the faith community. Neither underscores the faith-statement—essential to theology—that the positive function of ministry, of healing service to others, is heightened by a common belief in God's personal activity. They stress the importance of individuation and self-assertion rather than public identification with that community which shares the hope of the fulfillment of God's promises. They de-emphasize the community that is publicly called to share in God's revolutionary activity for man's liberation from oppression.

Secondly, they do not discuss the revolutionary role played by God in giving man new life in the resurrection. They stress what man can do, but not what a personal God does in liberating man. Resurrection brings violence and death into our life, but as conquered. The resurrection of the individual is an event in the future, but it may be anticipated. A share in the resurrection of Jesus augments a person's confidence that God will give man new life, in spite of his daimonic nature, and will fill him now with an inner conviction of dignity and worth ("power"). A recognition of God's role in the resurrection of each individual enables one to realize one's own transforming role in society. The individual no longer has to worry about the outcome: "O Death, where is your victory, O Death, where is your sting?" (1 Cor. 15:55) Each person is then free to aim for the ultimate salvation ("health") of all men.

Jung's comments on the origin and alleviation of suffering raise certain problems for further consideration. He states that "God" is a complex of ideas of an archetypal nature, having a reality independent of the conscious mind. This is a psychological view that neither affirms nor denies a personal God. When Jung was asked if he believed in God, he replied simply: "I know." How does this square with the theologian's God who liberates man and invites him to respond to the invitation to create the future in partnership? Again, regarding Christ, Jung does not feel that the personal historical life of Jesus is as important as his mythical life. Jesus' uniqueness is that he serves as the response of God to the problem of suffering, that is, in the incarnation He is the symbol, the center, the definitive instance of individuation, of what every man may become. But is this the theologian's concern: Jesus of Nazareth (an historical person with the human condition) who was also the God-man (what every person can become)? Thirdly, Jung sees evil, reduced to its ontological roots, as an aspect or name for God. He denies the patristic notion of evil as a privation of good, and gives it an eternal existence alongside God. Does naming the daimonic in order to conquer it actually achieve this goal? Fourthly, Jung feels that a person can become an integrated individual by following his dreams and by being aware of the unconscious. But aren't a person's social and political dimensions also important: how can a person become healthy without healing others, that is, how can a person have inner freedom without external peace?

The theologian's difficulty with Jung is often that they each communicate in a different language. His problem with May is that May understands the theologian's language but too often interprets it in his own way. For example, May rightly characterizes Christ as a rebel. Though he takes pains to distinguish the rebel from the revolutionary in order to show the liberating role of Jesus in calling man to realize his significance and worth, May will inevitably upset those who view Jesus as perfect and unchanging from the first moment of his existence. Also, May talks of the necessity of violence for growth and self-esteem. He sees violence as a way of overcoming powerlessness in society, of establishing contact between individuals. The person who is geared to active nonviolence, however, will deny all violence and downgrade its positive life-creating value. Thirdly, May says that if power is rejected, powerlessness becomes a virtue. Power is a reality with an energy that May wants to channel and temper with love. There are people however, who say that all power corrupts, and that power can be had only by taking it from someone else. These people will not admit that giving power to others or sharing it with them is itself a sign of power and strength. Finally, many criticize May for insisting on the use of power and violence because they feel that violence can be used by an oppressor to perpetuate an unjust situation or even by those well-intentioned people who think they are acting in the best interests of others when they are actually causing more harm than good. It is precisely to avoid such pseudo-innocence and self-deception that May is so careful to stress the role of the transcendent and the importance of compassion.

The Contribution to Liberation Theology

Jung and May do not stress the role of the church or the role of God in the resurrection. Moreover they raise problems of communication and misunderstanding. Yet both psychoanalysts make an important contribution to a theology of liberation.

They both stress a strong healthy self-image. In an age where many turn to the occult or to a Western version of mysticism for identity, they underscore the importance of increased self-awareness, and of using one's creativity. Their emphasis on knowing the self goes beyond an appreciation of the laws of evolution, to an understanding of the necessity of struggle for each person to become what he is called to be.

They are both eschatological. They recognize that man lives in a transitional age and brings the new era of the Spirit closer by confirming and confronting the transcendent. The process of becoming human is the gradual emergence and clarification of something that was already there—call it wholeness, call it the power of self-esteem, call it the divine. It will only come through violence and apocalyptic destruction of all present oppression and injustice. Man is a person who is "on the way," steadily moving toward his divine as well as his human goal.

Both are more concerned with transcending the daimonic rather than eliminating it. The daimonic is manifested in evil and violent acts. It is transcended when a person realizes the place of evil in his process of growth. Jesus had to undergo his suffering on the cross before resurrection was possible. Thus evil is transcended when a person accepts the responsibility for his ethical decision-making and refuses to deny guilt by foisting it off on the devil. It is transcended when a person recognizes the need of a savior and realizes that divine help or grace is offered and available in every situation, no matter how powerful the destructive forces.

Finally, both Jung and May emphasize the possibility of liberation. Liberation is the recognition of one's ability to be a "thou" rather than an "it," to say "yes" in spite of daimonic forces which tend to restrain a person from saying either "yes" or "no." It is a confidence that a process of redemption (wholeness) will emerge from the refusal to conform to the world, to fate, to the given. It is not only freedom from oppression, but freedom for growth. Liberation then, is the conscious awareness that each has the dignity and ability to develop his own personality not apart from suffering, but in the midst of it. At this juncture the psychologist and the theologian share the same vision.

Notes

1. For an excellent general survey of the various positions, see Eric Fromm, *The Anatomy of Human Destructiveness* (New York: Holt, Rinehart, and Winston, 1972), as well as Harry Kaufmann, *Aggression and Altruism* (New York: Holt, Rinehart, and Winston, 1970). Also, see the articles by E. I. Megargee, "The Psychology of Violence: a critical review of Theories of Violence," prepared for the U.S. National Commission on the Causes and Prevention of Violence, Task Force III: Individual Acts of Violence. See also Morton T. Kelsey, "Aggression and Religion: The Psychology and Theology of the Punitive Element in Man," *Religious Education* 68 (1973), pp. 366–386.

2. Cf. Sigmund Freud, *Beyond the Pleasure Principle*, Standard Edition, vol. 18 (1920), and *Civilization and Its Discontents*, trans. James Strachey (New York: W. W. Norton & Co., 1961). See also Konrad Lorenz, *On Aggression* (New York: Harcourt, Brace, and Jovanovitch, 1966), as well as books by his disciples Desmond Morris, *The Naked Ape* (New York: McGraw-Hill, 1967) and I. Eibl-Eibesfelt, *On Love and Hate: the Natural History of Behavior Patterns*, trans. G. Strachan (New York: Holt, Rinehart, and Winston, 1972).

3. Eric Fromm, *op cit.*, and Harry Kaufmann, *op. cit.*, both have extensive criticism of the classical positions before developing their own theories.

4. Cf. John Dollard and Neal Miller, et al., *Frustration and Aggression* (New Haven: Yale University Press, 1939) as well as *Personality and Psychotherapy* (New York: McGraw-Hill, 1950). Other writings in this area would include Anthony Storr, *Human Aggression* (New York: Atheneum, 1968); B. F. Skinner, *Beyond Freedom and Dignity* (New York: Knopf, 1971), and *Science and Human Behavior* (New York: Macmillan, 1953); and Leonard Berkowitz, *The Roots of Aggression: A Re-examination of the Frustration-Aggression Hypothesis* (New York: Atherton, 1969).

5. I am drawing from the latest writings of Rollo May, *Power and Violence* (New York: W. W. Norton & Co., 1972), and *Love and*

Will (New York, Delta Books, 1969). The sources from C. G. Jung are *Memories, Dreams, and Reflections* (New York: Vintage Books, 1965) and the seventeen volumes of the *Collected Works*, published by The Bollingen Foundation XX (New York, Pantheon Books). Hereafter, I will just cite the particular volume. Of particular interest are: Vol. 9,I, *The Archetypes and the Collective Unconscious*; Vol. 9,II, *Aion*; Vol. 11, *Psychology and Religion: West and East*; and Vol. 14, *Mysterium Conjunctionis*.

6. For his discussion on *privatio boni*, cf. *Aion* (9,II:49–52; 266–269) as well as *Answer to Job* (11:357–358).

7. The devil gets his due in several places, e.g., "A Psychological Approach to the Dogma of the Trinity" (11:168–169) and *Civilization in Transition* (10:456–466).

8. For more on the shadow, one of Jung's basic concepts, cf. "The Fight with the Shadow" (10:218–244) and *Aion* (9,II:8–10).

9. These notes on collective evil as manifestation of man's shadow or unconscious come in particular from "The Undiscovered Self" (10:219,222,260); *Mysterium Conjunctionis* (14:183); and "After the Catastrophe" (10:198–200). Stanley Milgram, *Obedience to Authority* (New York: Harper & Row, 1973), in describing various experiments with subjects on an electric shock generator, shows to what extent persons will obey an individual in punishing another human being when ordered to do so by a seemingly competent authority. Some subjects continued to administer severe shocks to a patient (actually an accomplice of Milgram) even after he had faked a catatonic fit. The reactions are well summarized by one subject: "So he's dead . . . I did my job."

10. May has a much more thorough discussion of the daimonic in chapters 5 and 6 of *Love and Will*.

11. *Power and Innocence*, p. 44. Cf. also, p. 182 and *Love and Will*, pp. 30–31. Here I am using violence and aggression interchangeably even though May is careful to distinguish them: "Aggression is object-oriented—that is, we know at whom and what we are angry. But in violence, the object-relation disintegrates, and we swing wildly, hitting whoever is in range" (*Power and Innocence*, p. 183).

12. *Ibid.*, p. 185. Cf. also *Love and Will*, pp. 158–159.

13. *Answer to Job* (11:417).

14. Cf. *The Undiscovered Self* (10:297) and *Answer to Job* (11:467).

15. This psychic wholeness, or individuation, goes by different names and different symbols: in the West we would say Christ instead of "self"; in the Near East it would be Khidr; in the Far East atman or Tao or the Buddha. In all cases, "self" means psychic wholeness.

16. In other words, Jesus was oppressed and He identified with suffering. Because God raised him from the dead and gave him a new life, every person who now identifies with suffering (the cross) also has the assurance of overcoming that suffering (the resurrection).

17. Note that Jung considers that Jesus became divine at the moment he despaired on the cross: at that moment he confronted himself, and his human nature attained divinity; at that moment God experienced what it meant to be a mortal man and drank to the dregs what he made his faithful servant Job suffer. This supreme moment is as divine as it is human, as "eschatological" as it is "psychological." Cf. *Answer to Job* (11:408); also "A Psychological Approach to the Dogma of the Trinity" (11:154–157) and "Christ, Symbol of the Self" (9,II:36–70).

18. *Power and Innocence*, p. 231. Jung has the same thought in his comments on the trickster: "If at the end of the Trickster myth, the savior is hinted at, this comforting premonition or hope means that some calamity or other has happened and been consciously understood. Only out of disaster can the longing for the savior arise—in other words, the recognition and unavoidable integration of the shadow create such a harrowing situation that nobody but a savior can undo the tangled web of fate." ("On the Psychology of the Trickster-Figure", 9,I:271).

19. *Ibid.*, p. 97; Cf. also, p. 243. May recognizes that violence also requires for its triggering some promise, a despair combined with the hope that conditions cannot but be better by one's own pain or death.

20. *Ibid.*, pp. 192–3, *passim*. Here he is following the thought of Frantz Fanon, especially in his book, *The Wretched of the Earth* (New York: Grove Press, 1965).

21. *Ibid.*, p. 250; cf. also p. 118.

22. *Ibid.*, pp. 216–217, 251–253 *passim*, and 260. In *Love and Will*, May prefers the term "care" to compassion, the state of being rather than the emotion.

IV CRITICISMS OF LIBERATION THEOLOGY

Jacques Ellul: A Christian Perspective on Revolution

JAMES GAFFNEY

Such topical phrases as "Christianity and revolution" are, in the current idiom of American theology, already clichés. Especially as a result of the recent popularity of what has come to be called liberation theology and of the widespread interest only a few years previously in Christian-Marxist eirenics, revolutionary phraseology has come to sound comfortably harmonious with the religious vocabulary of Christians. So quickly, however, do novelties turn into banalities nowadays, that we may have to strain our memories to appreciate just how quickly our theological fashions do change, and thereby arrive at a valid appreciation of just when, where, and with whom the most original and seasoned thinking on a given subject actually took place. For it is not at all long ago that Christianity and revolution would have struck most people as unrelated ideas if not positively incompatible interests. I stress this point in the context of this essay because, where there is certainly nothing remarkable about the fact that in the 1970's Jacques Ellul explored the relationship between Christianity and revolution, it is distinctly remarkable that he did so almost forty years ago. In 1936 he published an article in *Le semeur* under the title "Christianisme et révolution," and in

1948 a major portion of what is probably the most basic of his books, that which is called in English *The Presence of the Kingdom*, was entitled *Le Christianisme, puissance révolutionnaire.* Ellul, in other words, was devoting himself very seriously to this topic long before the bandwagon had even begun to roll. And that alone seems to me good reason for singling him out for notice.

There is also another reason, no less persuasive. To write theologically about revolution is obviously a different kind of undertaking than theologizing about the Trinity, or the Atonement, or the theological virtues. It is not that revolution is a more important or more difficult subject, but that it is a much more contingent one. For that reason it is a kind of subject unlikely to be illuminated by thinkers whose orientation is exclusively theoretical and abstract. One tends to view sheerly academic reflections on revolution with the same lack of confidence as, say, celibate views on sexual intimacy. Moreover, even within a theoretical perspective, revolution is derived not from theological but from political experience, and its intelligibility involves among other things a better than ordinary understanding of the workings of law, and of those social conflicts which law proves, in fact if not in theory, incompetent to resolve. Such considerations may incline one to consider with more than usual interest a theological writer who addresses revolution and who has been a French Resistance fighter, a champion of Algerians' rights against oppressive policies and practices, a deputy mayor of a large commercial and industrial city, a lawyer, and a university professor of Law and Government. Such a background would seem decidedly helpful for adopting the procedure which Gustavo Gutierrez calls "critical reflection on praxis." [1] At the very least, whatever the possessor of such credentials may have to say on this subject can scarcely be dismissed as mere armchair theorizing.

And yet, anyone who reads Jacques Ellul expecting to

hear some prophetic clarion call for Christians to fling themselves into great revolutionary movements is sure to be disappointed. In book after book of his we find Christian participation in such movements questioned and even denounced, while to stand aloof from them seems often to be the only position he considers appropriate for Christians. This impression is one that needs both refinement and explanation, but even at face value it carries an important implication for one's evaluation of Jacques Ellul. Namely, he obviously is not what certain devotees of liberation theology are: a mere recruiter of Christians to revolutionary causes for whose approval or adoption Christian convictions are in no way essential. Very often nowadays revolutionary concerns are urged upon Christians as common causes which transcend the differences between Christian and non-Christian people. We are all familiar with the appeal that Christians work shoulder to shoulder with atheistic Communists on behalf of human values which both groups hold dear. That kind of collaboration pleases many of us not only by its efficiency in combining alienated human resources, but also by its capacity to counteract that narrowly sectarian mentality whose unlovely spiritual profile has been depicted in unflattering detail by modern social psychology. The success of a character like Archie Bunker as one of America's outstanding cultural buffoons indicates that an insular mentality of bigotry and exclusiveness is, if not more uncommon, at least more embarrassing to our contemporaries than it seems to have been to our ancestors. And the current widespread eagerness to unite Christians with unbelievers in mutually valued moral enterprises is in part a healthy symptom of that embarrassment.

Whatever value we may attach to this sort of thing, it is not unfair to say that Jacques Ellul takes little or no interest in it, and that the tone in which he refers to Christian identification with secular causes is usually sceptical or hostile. His scepticism and hostility, however, are by no means the uncritical and spontaneous reaction of crude prejudice. They are religiously motivated and theologically reasoned. In order to appreciate his point of view as sympathetically as possible, we need to recall that the current enthusiasm for active cooperation in common concerns between Christians and non-Christians at times carries questionable implications. Proposals to "set aside our differences" are often equated with "rising above our differences" or even "our petty differences," thus gradually strengthening a suggestion that the differences are situated on a lower plane of values than the likenesses. And for any theologian the assumption that what distinguishes Christians from others is less important than what does not must be either an actually heretical idea or at least a problematic one. After all, what makes this difference is supposed to be the "pearl of great price," the great "gift of God," to which anything and everything else, including life itself, may be sacrificed without extravagance. No one can seriously doubt that this is traditional, biblically founded Christian belief, and it is hard to see how anyone who really holds it can consider behavior which boasts of "transcending" the differences between Christians and non-Christians as the very highest type of behavior.

Whenever one discusses this sort of thing among Christians, an objection is eventually raised: In the abstract, Christianity may represent the highest values, but the same cannot be maintained in the concrete of those who call themselves Christians in contrast with those who do not. Hence we have the recently popular idea of the "anonymous Christian"—which should perhaps be accompanied by some complementary idea of the anonymous non-Christian. And of course there are possibilities of endless rhetoric about there being more "real" Christianity among those who do not identify themselves as Christian than among those who do. Moreover, this idea too can lay claim to an impressive, if rather more subtle tradition, and it is certainly not without theological respectability. Nevertheless, one should not naively suppose that Jacques Ellul is any less aware of this than the rest of us. For regardless of who the "real" Christians may happen to be—an identification presumably best left to God—the distinction between them and the "real" non-Christians remains a meaningful one, and indeed an indispensable one for preserving the very intelligibility of large areas of Christian theology, including just about all the theology of Jacques Ellul.

It is highly characteristic of Ellul's thought to be habitually conscious of and frequently insistent upon what we may call Christian theological dualism. What I mean by this is that pattern of a profound duality with which the New Testament abounds, and which is perhaps most conspicuously expressed in the Johannine writings, even if its impact on later theology has been more often mediated by the writings of St. Paul. There is no need to belabor this point—the sheep and the goats, the children of light and the children of darkness, Christ and Antichrist, the Spirit and the flesh, the Kingdom and the World, are familiar examples of a pervasive motif without which few Christians could say anything at all about divine judgment or divine redemption. And yet, of course, theologians of a certain kind have recurrently exhibited a certain genius for eliminating this seemingly indispensable element of the faith, thereby producing a version of Christianity in which, as Richard Niebuhr describes it, "a God without wrath brought men without sin into a kingdom without judgment through the ministrations of a Christ without a cross." [2]

It would seem to be the fear of that kind of perversion of the gospel which prompts Ellul in nearly all his theological writings to dwell on the difference between the Kingdom and the World, understanding the former as the eschatological reign of God and the latter in the pejorative sense characteristic of the Fourth Gospel. His view of the relationship between Kingdom and World is basic to his theology as a whole as well as to his reflections on the relationship between Christianity, politics, and more specifically between Christianity and revolution.

Ellul's emphasis on the profound discrepancy between Kingdom and World does not imply Christian indifference to the World or flight from it. His theology allows no room at all for ecclesiastical isolationism, and compels him to conclude that "to speak of an 'evangelizing Church' is to indulge in a tautology, for if there is no mission to the World there is no Church." [3] Thus the first of his books to deal extensively with our topic was originally entitled *Présence au monde moderne*, where the French clarifies what the English conceals, namely that *The Presence of the Kingdom* is conceived as an active force, whose objective is precisely the World. Nevertheless, the fact that fifteen years later he published a closely related book, called in English *False Presence of the Kingdom*, underscores a growing awareness that the Kingdom's presence to the World is susceptible to contrary interpretations. For although it is evident to readers of the earlier book that he was conscious of this problem from the start,[4] developments between 1948 and 1963 moved him to deal with it directly and in detail. Accordingly, on the first page of the earlier work we find him insisting that "the Christian has not been created in order to separate himself from or live aloof from the world," [5] but the later book opens with a simple acknowledgement that "Christians in our day have become aware of a great truth: that the Church cannot live turned in upon herself and for herself." [6] Clearly, then, he feels that the point of the former book, the active calling of Christianity vis-à-vis the World, has not been ignored but rather misconstrued and misapplied. The respective themes of these two books, positive and hortatory in the one, negative and cautionary in the other, represent the opposite terms of a dialectical pattern which characterizes a great deal of

Ellul's thought, especially on the political and revolutionary aspects of the Church.

Even in his earliest statements on "revolutionary Christianity" Ellul makes it clear that he regards revolution as an equivocal term. This idea is developed at length in *Autopsy of Revolution*, published in French in 1969. The main distinction Ellul wishes to emphasize is between revolution as an intense acceleration of already existing trends, and revolution as the contravening of present social tendencies. It is the latter idea which Ellul considers to be the original and authentic one. Hence the prototypical revolutionary sentiment is that matters have been allowed to go so far in a given direction that a stop must be put to them. Revolution begins in revolt, and what revolt expresses is on the one hand exasperation, a sense of the intolerable, and on the other hand accusation, a conviction of injustice. What follows revolt is a struggle to resist and reverse a direction of events which can no longer be endured. However, under the influence of Hegelian and Marxist philosophies, "revolution literally changed character in the nineteenth century. Thereafter it was directed towards a practical future, an attempted fusion of the old conflicting forces, and a new synthesis of society." [7] In this view, "revolution is a function of the maturation or the maturity of a society." [8]

Just as, contrary to this view, resistance and reversal of actual developments are for Ellul characteristics of genuine revolution, so too are they characteristics of the only kind of revolution he is willing to qualify as Christian. The revolutionary force of Christianity means for him exclusively a force of resistance to establish patterns of development. Thus Ellul finds totally unacceptable all theories which, one way or another, subsume the revolutionary aspects of Christianity under a basic evolutionary or "process" pattern, as for instance those constructed to harmonize with the thought of Teilhard de Chardin whose more original contributions Ellul regards as theologically unsound.

Revolutionary Christianity means for Ellul that active Christian presence which entails an element of resolute and strenuous opposition to certain tendencies prevailing in the World. The opposition arises from perceiving these tendencies as incompatible with the Kingdom, where to proclaim the Kingdom in word and deed, as every Christian is required to do, simply entails striving against them. But if the true presence of the Kingdom involves revolutionary aspects, so too, unfortunately, does its false presence. And Ellul is increasingly preoccupied with ill-advised revolutionary participation on the part of Christians as a principal way in which the false presence of the Kingdom is extended.

The presence of the Kingdom, according to Ellul's reading of the New Testament, is essentially revolutionary. Its initial spirit is one of revolt, exasperation and accusation, and its subsequent course is one of revolution, resistance and conflict. What this revolt and ensuing revolution are against is, in general, the World. This is, of course, a very comprehensive theological concept, which is applied concretely and practically by different people in very different ways. The more familiar elements of biblical vocabulary equate it with a realm of sin and death, enslavement to the flesh, subjection to satanic power. Traditional Christian theology transmits these ideas mainly within the framework of original sin as developed in the anti-Pelagian controversy. More recent theology replaces that framework with such reinterpretations as that of the "sin of the world" or with various sociological and psychological conceptions of corporate guilt or collective oppression. For Ellul, it is this World, however one chooses to label it, which is the sole objective of authentically Christian revolution.

However Ellul does not see the World merely as a kind of mythological designation for human misbehavior, proceeding from wickedness or folly, and the trouble it causes in society. He clearly attaches much more than rhetorical significance to the Pauline assertion that our struggle is not against flesh and blood but against principalities and powers. In some sense not altogether clear to me, he certainly believes in a spiritual dominion of evil representing truly daimonic influence, of which the observable facts of injustice and the suffering it entails are merely the manifestation. His Calvinist heritage is prominent in this regard, and he has unconcealed contempt for ideas in Catholic theology which suggest a kind of middle ground of natural goodness intermediate between the realms of sin and grace. In Ellul's thought, "He who is not with me is against me" evidently requires no qualifications whatsoever, and a philosophy which admits the natural perfectibility of man, not hypothetically but actually, ranks as a pernicious illusion.

Ellul's eschatology is both immanentist and apocalyptic. That is, he recognizes both realized eschatology, the historical actuality of the Kingdom, and future eschatology, the triumphant eventuality of the Kingdom. The revolutionary aspect of Christianity belongs to the realm of realized eschatology, the confrontation of the World with the gospel of the Kingdom.

It is at this point that the problem arises which has occupied Ellul in recent years. It consists in the fact that the Christian's opposition to the World inevitably overlaps with other patterns of opposition. Consequently, the Christian revolution has a way of getting allied with, and ultimately confused with other revolutions of a quite different kind. Christians, for example, are irrevocably committed to love their neighbors and to actively express that love in the pursuit of social justice. They are therefore irrevocably opposed to political and economic oppression. Suppose, then, that Christians find themselves in the presence of Fascist oppression, for example. They must condemn it, and must oppose it, otherwise, they betray not only the sufferers of oppression but their very faith. But once they undertake to oppose it, they are likely to find themselves in uneasy alliance with others who oppose it on quite different grounds. The Christian adversary of a Fascist oppressor might find Marxist adversaries of that same Fascist oppressor. And the fact that in numbers there is strength constitutes a powerful inducement to join forces.

So far, so good. But the consequences of this concerted action, and even more of its victorious outcome, can be very dangerous to Christianity. The danger appears most clearly in two respects. First, Christians who side with non-Christians and even anti-Christians against oppression frequently discover that what they are abetting is not the elimination of oppression, but merely the replacement of one oppressor by another. Power corrupts. It corrupts socialists as well as capitalists, and dictatorships of the proletariat have a way of turning out just as autocratic and ruthless as dictatorships of the aristocracy or bourgeoisie. Thus what is envisioned as a struggle between the Kingdom and the World might merely serve the purposes of some redistribution of power within the World, and the displacement of one worldly ideology by another.

Secondly, the very whole-heartedness with which Christians collaborate with non-Christians in struggles against evil often leads Christians to identify their effort so completely with the ideology of their allies that their real Christian identity becomes confused with that ideology, subordinated to it, and ultimately consumed by it. It is not uncommon, for instance, to hear Christianity identified with the cause of anti-Communism. A good many of us have *also* heard it preached in terms which made it virtually indistinguishable from Marxist revolutionary theory. All of us can certainly cite examples of both Marxist and anti-Communist victories equally repugnant to any genuinely Christian conscience.

The most recent elaboration of Ellul's thinking on this subject is in his book *Autopsy of Revolution*. Although this whole work is devoted to revolution, it is to only a limited extent a theological treatment of the subject, and I shall confine my consideration to that aspect. One portion is titled "The Theology of Revolution," [9] but the significance, or at least the spirit of this essay can be appreciated only if one observes that it is part of a larger section called "Vulgarized Revolution." [10] The dominant idea is that revolution has become an increasingly popular idea at the very same time that it has become a decreasingly lucid and consistent one. We are thus approaching a point in contemporary thought at which everybody will be in favor of revolution but nobody will know or care what a revolution is. Within such a context it is not surprising that "The Theology of Revolution" is essentially a diatribe, beginning on the rather sour note that "Christian intellectuals dabble in revolution." [11] And it concludes on the still sourer note that "the only thing they prove is that Christians adapt admirably to the impulses of society, and that revolution has become the most banal, puerile, and meaningless word in an endless stream of discourse." [12] Apart from heaping charges of misinformation, misinterpretation, and obscurantism upon a number of writers whose work he deplores (including the American, Richard Shaull), Ellul distinguishes "two main trends among modern Christian revolutionaries." [13] The first he interprets as follows: since revolutionary movements seem to be permanently recurring facts of modern life, whose service to social progress is generally acknowledged, Christianity, which has all too often found itself on the "wrong" sides of social disputes, seeks to redeem itself by becoming an unfailing, and therefore uncritical advocate of revolution. The second trend, for which the first prepares the way, is towards promoting revolution to a position of such unchallenged supremacy on the scale of moral values that it effectively eclipses Christian faith itself. None of this material is altogether new in Ellul's thought, but it is expressed here with unprecedented clarity. For earlier and cooler light on the subject, one does well to refer to previous writings, including the two we have already mentioned and one other, *Violence: Reflections from a Christian Perspective.*[14]

At the risk of some oversimplification, I would suggest that the main importance of violence in Ellul's view of revolution as I have been presenting it, is as a kind of touchstone, an instrument of discrimination. The more easily a Christian's revolutionary undertakings acquiesce in violence, the more certainly they can be categorized as the false presence of the Kingdom. Ellul has been rightly criticized for neglecting to provide an explicit and adequate definition of violence, but after reading his book one can, I think, at least approximate a definition he would approve. I shall define it as an unjust use of force against the innocent exercise of freedom, and while we can all think of examples that would make such a definition seem hazy, unequivocal examples are really all that Ellul needs. For while he excellently summarizes the variety of traditional Christian views on the use of violence, he considers it to be evident that violence, plain and simple, is utterly alien to the Kingdom and therefore consistently rejected by Jesus Christ. Accordingly, he pays special attention to the willingness of so many Christian revolutionaries reluctantly or enthusiastically to make use of violence, often under the illusion or pretext that it is an emergency measure which will be discreetly set aside after the revolution succeeds. According to Ellul, the only proper Christian response is to reject the violence of others, and to repent for violence of one's own. Consistent with this view, Ellul honors the nonviolent resistance of Martin Luther King as authentically Christian and revolutionary, and sees his work (and, interestingly enough, Gandhi's as well) as the presence of the Kingdom. It is likewise consistent that he pays a kind of

intellectual "devil's due" respect also to Rap Brown and
Stokely Carmichael who, judging violence to be indispensable, judged Christianity to be consequently untenable.
Their kind of revolution belongs to the World, and makes
no pretenses about it. What Ellul despises as the false
presence of the Kingdom is the desire to have both the Cross
and the Sword. To those who object saying "Look at what
happened to Martin Luther King," his response is double-
edged. As far as the World is concerned, he suggests "Look
at what happened to Malcolm X." And as far as the
Kingdom is concerned he suggests "Look at what happened
to Jesus Christ." Death is not the point, but whether or not
out of death comes life. Death is the World's business. Life is
the Kingdom's. Death is their meeting point. Life is their
divergence.

The kind of touchstone violence represents is also evidenced by a number of other things which test the
authenticity of Christian revolution. For example, do the
revolutionaries seek justice only in popular ideological
causes, or in unpopular non-ideological ones as well? And
do they only join with well established struggles or do they
also make the lonely, unpublicized beginnings of resistance?
When struggles are over and tables are turned, does their
justice and compassion extend as generously to the van-
quished as it did to the victors? Does the love of enemies
embrace even those whose hostility is directed to the
revolution itself and to cherished ideologies? It is in such
terms as these that the Christian revolutionary is invited to
exercise his discernment of spirits.

And finally, his ultimate striving must be against not this
or that social, political, or ideological group, but against the
instrumentalities of sin and death that cut across all party
lines. It is in the development of this theme that Ellul
fashions his well-known critiques of money-centredness,
technocracy, propaganda, nationalism, and other institutions of modern life which he believes foster the World's

realm of sin and death and most urgently require the presence of the Kingdom.[15]

As a Christian theologian, it is the theological, rather than the social or economic or political point of Ellul's work on revolution that concerns me, and I have tried not to stray too far from that point. I have subtitled this essay "A Christian Perspective on Revolution" because it seems to me that the most important thing about Ellul's view of this subject is his insistence that a Christian perspective on revolution is, in the last analysis, a unique perspective: that it is not and cannot be identical with any other. As Ellul sees it, Christianity is revolutionary, but in its own way and for its own reasons. That way depends on the reasons, and can find no sufficient justification apart from them. But since those reasons are reasons of faith, they can be thoroughly shared only in the sharing of faith. And the faith in question is not in man, or technological progress, or political efficiency, or social enlightenment. It is not faith in the World. It is faith in God who raised Jesus Christ from the dead. The Christian therefore confronts the World with his faith, that is both his gift and his mission. In respecting his mission, the Christian must offer his faith to the World—display it, proclaim it, commend it. But at the very same time, in respecting his gift, the Christian must defend his faith against the World—preserve it, cherish it, keep it intact. To the extent that the World accepts the gift of faith it ceases to be the World, and becomes the Kingdom. To the extent that the World rejects that gift it becomes more than ever the World. At that point, the Christian's confrontation with the World must be transformed from appeal to intransigence, from an assertion of the Kingdom's truth to a rejection of the World's lie, and from a labor of evangelism to an ordeal of martyrdom. In Ellul's terms, to undertake that labor and to undergo that ordeal precisely constitute the presence of the Kingdom, whereas to reject either the one or the other while at the same time claiming to be

Christian constitutes the false presence of the Kingdom. These are the alternatives which present themselves with respect to revolution, just as they present themselves in every domain of interaction between the Kingdom and the World. And always, when Kingdom and World cease to be distinguishable from one another by what they say and what they do, we may be quite sure that one has yielded to and has been assimilated by the other. Jacques Ellul insists that we ask "Which one?"

Notes

1. Gustave Gutierrez, *A Theology of Liberation* (Maryknoll: Orbis, 1973), pp. 6ff.

2. H. Richard Niebuhr, *The Kingdom of God in America* (New York: Harper & Row, 1973), p. 193.

3. Jacques Ellul, *False Presence of the Kingdom* (New York: Seabury, 1972), p. 1.

4. Jacques Ellul, *The Presence of the Kingdom* (New York: Seabury, 1967), e.g., p. 16.

5. *Ibid.,* p. 7.

6. *False Presence of the Kingdom,* p. 1.

7. Jacques Ellul, *Autopsy of Revolution* (New York: Knopf, 1971), p. 117.

8. *Ibid.,* p. 118.

9. *Ibid.,* pp. 217–233.

10. *Ibid.,* ch. 4.

11. *Ibid.,* p. 217.

12. *Ibid.,* p. 232.

13. *Ibid.,* p. 221.

14. Jacques Ellul, *Violence: Reflections from a Christian Perspective* (New York: Seabury, 1969).

15. All of Ellul's books thus far published in English have some bearing on this theme. The following is a list of them: *Autopsy of Revolution* (New York: Knopf, 1971), *Critique of the New Commonplaces* (New York: Knopf, 1968), *False Presence of the Kingdom* (New York: Seabury, 1972), *Hope in Time of Abandonment* (New York: Seabury, 1973), *The Judgment of Jonah* (Grand Rapids: Eerdmans,

1971), *The Meaning of the City* (Grand Rapids: Eerdmans, 1970), *Political Illusion* (New York: Knopf, 1967), *The Politics of God and the Politics of Man* (Grand Rapids: Eerdmans, 1972), *Prayer and Modern Man* (New York: Seabury, 1973), *Propaganda: The Formation of Men's Attitudes* (New York: Random, 1973), *The Presence of the Kingdom* (New York: Seabury, 1967), *The Technological Society* (New York: Knopf, 1964), *The Theological Foundation of Law* (New York: Seabury, 1969), *To Will and To Do* (Philadelphia: Pilgrim, 1969), *Violence: Reflections from a Christian Perspective* (New York: Seabury, 1969).

Liberation Theology in the Thought of Gustaf Wingren

FRANCIS J. REILLY

G. K. Chesterton once told a parable about two small boys, playing in their yard, to whom a wandering genie gave the opportunity to become whatever they wished. The first boy, who chose to become a giant, soon discovered that all the things of the earth, even mountains and oceans, had become as small and insignificant as the stones and puddles in his yard. The second boy, who chose to become as small as he possibly could be, discovered that the things of his yard, such as stones and puddles, had become as awesome and fascinating as mountains and oceans. The first boy died of boredom, the second lived happily ever after.[1]

One might dispute this parable; still there is much to be said for being small, at least in the sense of appreciating the greatness and the significance of the everyday world before one's eyes. Thus, among the theological personae there is much to be said for Gustaf Wingren. At the beginning of his career as a student, long before he succeeded Anders Nygren as Professor of systematic theology at the University of Lund and became the leading figure in the new generation of Swedish theologians, Wingren pledged himself to the integration of the Christian faith and ordinary, everyday life. During a scholarly career that has spanned the last thirty years, he has pursued that goal with remarkable determination and consistency. In this pursuit Wingren has been involved in a variety of topical theological discussions, including the current controversy over liberation theology. The following remarks concern his contribution to this particular discussion. First, I will elucidate Wingren's fundamental theological concepts that explain his acceptance, in certain situations, of revolutionary activity; secondly, I will discuss his generally negative comments concerning liberation theology; and finally, I will provide a positive statement of liberation theology constructed primarily on the basis of Wingren's fundamental theological concepts.

Fundamental Concepts

The starting point of Wingren's theology is *creation*, the dynamic reality of life in all its aspects: birth, bodily existence in the external world, human community, the primary needs of life such as food, shelter and clothing, and the primary occupations directed toward the satisfaction of these needs.[2] All of these ordinary, everyday realities have to do with God's act of creation and the reception of life from Him. The final goal is the union of human persons with God in Christ, in Whose image we are all created. In a sense this union was given at the beginning of time. Adam came from the hand of God as a child, called to grow at one and the same time into human maturity and into the image and likeness of God.[3]

The project of growth has been disrupted by the entrance of sin into the world. All of us, in Adam, are bound by Satan, estranged from God, in conflict with the earth and with one another. In this sinful situation, God addresses creation with the word of the *law*. First the law preserves creation by demanding and compelling the performance of external works which satisfy the bodily needs of the human community. Secondly the law accuses and condemns the individual for his failure to meet God's demands, or for his sinfully selfish fulfillment of them.[4] This notion of the law is clearly stated in traditional Lutheranism. But there the law is equated almost totally with the civil authority and its power to coerce and punish. Wingren accepts this authority as one manifestation of the law but he insists that the concept be broadened to include all those forces in life which place demands upon us and accuse us of failure. The first use of the law concerns our relationship with our neighbors; the second use concerns our feelings of guilt and the reality of death.[5]

The law is the word of God but not the word which He wants to speak. It is an alien word wrung from Him by the need to restrain and to punish the alien reality of sin. In His proper word, the word of the *gospel*, God triumphs over the alien word of the law. Wingren emphasizes that the word of the gospel has a twofold meaning: it includes both the forgiveness of sins and the promise of life. Both aspects of the gospel were conveyed to the people of Palestine by Jesus in a somewhat limited fashion because Jesus Himself was a man under the law, subject to its demands and its condemnation. But Jesus properly fulfilled the demands of the law and totally accepted its condemnation, thus accomplishing in His own being victory over the law and the recapitulation of creation, i.e., the restoration of its original, sinless state and the consummation of its growth to perfection and into union with God. Now, risen from the dead, He is present in the world, extending to the men of all times and places the word of forgiveness and the promise of life.[6]

All of this might sound common, but it approaches a very un-Lutheran view of the gospel. Theologians as widely separated in time and orientation as Martin Luther and Rudolf Bultmann emphasize one aspect of the gospel: the word of forgiveness. Wingren criticizes both men, and Lutheran theology in general, for unbiblical onesidedness.

The gospel, he insists, has an effect on the body. The miracles of Jesus are not mere illustrations of forgiveness but offers of the gift of life.[7]

Here we find ourselves face to face with the source of Wingren's "everyday" theology: a Jesus who considered it an essential aspect of His mission to answer the ordinary bodily needs of the people of His day.[8] Wingren's notion of salvation is not, however, social gospel Christianity. The consummation of recapitulation will be accomplished only in the resurrection of the dead. Nothing shows this more graphically than the miracles of Jesus. Those he fed hungered again, the blind he cured one day lost their sight, and the dead he raised eventually were buried. So also in today's world, the word of the gospel comes from One who is beyond death but to the billions who, being still in the flesh and under the law, still must experience it. The world is falling apart and passing away, and no indestructible life will come to the body until all that has died is raised to life.[9]

The decisive truth in this regard, however, is not the negative statement about present possibilities but the positive proclamation that the body, too, is saved. In the present time as in the time of Jesus there must be repeated manifestations of this bodily salvation. Thus the Church, which is taken from the world in order to return to it bearing the gospel, has a twofold purpose: to preach to all mankind the word of forgiveness and to perform for the whole of man the work of ministry,[10] and to devote itself to the task of healing, through the performances of all those works which protect human life against whatever forces seek to destroy it.[11]

Such a function demands that the Church exhibit a special concern for the weak and the oppressed, whose lives are most threatened.[12] And such a concern immediately raises a problem for the Church, because the defense of the weak can sometimes be accomplished only by the use of force, which many people consider contradictory to the

Christian commitment. Wingren's response to this problem is that God Himself, when He uses the alien word of the law, does that which might be considered contradictory to his nature; but in so doing God prepares men to hear the gospel. His alien work, therefore, serves His proper work. So also, the call of the Church to spread the gospel does not forbid but actually requires that Christians use force, when it is necessary, to restrain sin and to help the weak and the oppressed. When they do so, they do the work of God, whose wrath serves His love.[13]

The acceptance of the use of force requires of Christians the acceptance of certain "establishment" tasks, such as service in the army and with police forces. However, it also requires the acceptance of the responsibility to work for the abolition of unjust laws and to resist by whatever means necessary the oppressive activities of the tyrannical ruler. This is so because, as I mentioned earlier, Wingren considers the neighbor rather than the authority structure or the ruler the primary focus of the law. Thus, it is the need of the neighbor which has first claim upon us. Wingren, therefore, accepts what Luther absolutely rejected: the necessity and justifiability of Christian involvement in particular violent revolutionary movements.[14]

Comments on Revolution Theology

Having expressed himself in this way regarding the nature of the gospel and the task of the Church, Wingren might be sought in the front ranks of those who advocate a theology of revolution. As it happens, however, he has come down squarely on the other side of the debate, negatively judging liberation theology for the following reasons.

1. The motivation of liberation theology is suspect. It seems to be designed (as was the theology of orders of Nazi Germany), to meet the demands of contemporary culture and thus to preserve for the Church a position of influence.

If this really is the case, says Wingren, then in the whole of liberation theology there is not a single serious word.

2. Liberation theology is totally involved with change to the neglect of the nature of man. This involvement elevates a secondary question in theological anthropology to a position of primacy over the logically superior question.

3. The most common starting point of liberation theologies is Christocentric. But Christ is for all men; he cannot be enlisted into a cause, either conservative or radical.

4. Through the restrictive effect which it has on the image of Christ, liberation theology limits the number of people to whom the Church is open. Only if the Church is not forced to do service to a cause but is allowed to preach the word of the gospel to all can it be as Christ intends, the Church for the whole world.

5. The social gospel movement, which is closely related to liberation theology, is based on the assumption that the activity of ministry can accomplish great social changes and produce the kingdom of God on earth. Actually, as is shown by the example of the miracles of Jesus, it can only patch up what is passing away.[15]

Wingren's negative comments concerning liberation theology contain some points worth pondering. This theological movement, as any other, must constantly maintain a self-critical posture. Among the flaws which it must guard against are selfish motivation, concern with secondary matters, a possessive attitude toward Christ, divisive, exclusive ecclesiology and overconfidence in human possibilities. In short, the attempt to theologize about liberation must not end in theological bondage to liberation. Nevertheless, it seems to me that Wingren's comments are more negative than necessary and are also inconsistent with his fundamental theological concerns. On the basis of those concerns as well as on the basis of my own thoughts, I offer the following criticisms of his comments.

The attempt at relevance does not necessarily indicate

selfish motivation. Wingren himself insists that the Church must respond to the needs of human beings and, moreover, that it cannot wait for the "right" needs to arise before it sets itself to answer them. The Church must answer, as Christ does, the real needs that now exist.[16] Surely, a theology of revolution affirms this. Furthermore, it is obvious that liberation theology tends to alienate at least as many and perhaps more persons than it attracts (it might be added: more powerful persons), which indicates that its purpose is not to maintain a position of influence. Finally, if Wingren is correct and the motivation of this theology is selfish, the validity of its interpretation of the gospel is not thereby negated. The important thing, as Paul wrote, is that the gospel should be preached—for whatever reasons.[17]

The criticism of the exaltation of change to a position of primacy over the nature of man is consistent with Wingren's basic theological concern for the ordinary and the everyday. However, the need for change is in fact a large part of the ordinary, everyday situation of a great part of the human race. Wingren, when he criticizes those who are trying to alleviate that situation and occupy themselves with change, comes dangerously close to a retreat into the kind of conservatism which he himself deplores in nineteenth century Lutheranism and has described as nothing less than the opium of religion.[18]

It is difficult to understand how Wingren, who emphasizes the truth of God's law and recognizes the use of force to defend the weak, can object to the Christocentric basis of liberation theology. The almost certain implication is that Christ, in whom God and man are totally at one, has nothing to do with that coercion and violence which are appropriate to both God and man. Such a position effectively ignores not only the *communicatio idiomatum*, to which Wingren is intensely loyal,[19] but also the idea, stated clearly in the New Testament, that Christ the Servant is also the Judge and that the very special objects of His judgment will be 'those who trample the weak.[20] Kurt Vonnegut expresses this side of Christ in his story, "The Gospel from Outer Space." At the Resurrection, he tells us, God raised Jesus, who had been killed "safely" since he was a bum with no connections, made this bum his Son, giving him all the powers of the Ruler of the universe, and declared to the world the consequences of the event: From this day forward, anyone who kills a bum who has no connections will be punished horribly![21]

The Church, if it should espouse liberation theology, would not thereby limit the number of people to whom it is open. For centuries the oppressed have been members of the Church. As such, they often have been told to accept the inviolability of secular authority and to believe that the oppressions wrought by tyrannical rulers and institutions are the appropriate punishment for the sins of the people. Perhaps the time has come to preach the same message to a different audience, to tell those in authority and those who, by action or inaction, have supported these oppressive activities, that the revolutions of their subjects are visited upon them for the punishment of their sins, in the hope that by accepting this punishment they will be spared the wrath to come. Any and all of the powerful who can bear to hear that word and still remain in the Church are welcome to do so.

Wingren writes in another connection that one rarely finds the truth by inverting a lie.[22] Surely it must also be said that one does not properly respond to social gospel utopianism by dismissing human co-operation in the establishment of the kingdom. Nor is that co-operation less necessary because it can only put patches on a world that is falling apart. As Wingren maintains against Lutheran conservatism, Jesus was not discouraged from the performance of his miracles by the knowledge that their effect would be temporary.[23] Certainly, Christians should not believe that they can create a perfect world. Perhaps they must acknowledge as Luther did that no revolution ever created a society which did not, sooner or later, have a tragic end.[24] But if salvation really is bodily and if the future resurrection is to be manifested in the world by works of healing, then our works must include the work of patching up oppressive socio-political situations by whatever means appropriate and necessary.

A Positive Statement

In the first part of this essay I have demonstrated that the basic theological concepts of Gustaf Wingren lead inexorably to the acceptance, in certain situations, of violent revolutionary activity, and have indicated that Wingren's negative comments concerning liberation theology are to be taken seriously but are less than totally defensible. It is now time to construct a positive statement, on the basis of Wingren's own theological concepts, of liberation theology.

God, who creates people and who, when they sin, addresses to them the harsh word of the law, triumphs over that law with the offer, in Christ, of forgiveness and life. In the present age, God's people continue to experience the law; but they must experience also the effects of the gospel. Among the situations in which they experience the law and must experience the gospel is the sphere of politics. If, therefore, a political institution or a particular ruler become for any citizens a source of demand, condemnation and death to the exclusion of acceptance, forgiveness and life, those citizens have the right to reject that institution or ruler on their own behalf and for the sake of their neighbors. They may express this rejection in whatever form becomes necessary, including that of violent revolution. In such a revolution they manifest the presence of Christ, who is not only the Savior but the Judge who judges for the sake of saving. And in such a revolution they advance the mission of the Church to the world since the

Church, which brings to people the offer of forgiveness and life, also points out to them the sins for which they are forgiven and the death from which they shall be raised. All people, not only the weak and the oppressed but the powerful as well, must learn that in the present age they experience not only forgiveness and life but condemnation and death, which most fittingly come in a violent form to those who deny to others the experience of life.

Notes

1. Gilbert K. Chesterton, *Tremendous Trifles* (New York: Dodd, Mead and Co., 1910), 1–4.

2. G. Wingren, *Creation and Law*, trans. Ross MacKenzie (Philadelphia: Fortress Press, 1961), 98–99, 119; hereafter cited as *CL*. G. Wingren, *Theology in Conflict*, trans. Eric Wahlstrom (Philadelphia: Muhlenberg Press, 1958), 114.

3. G. Wingren, *Man and the Incarnation*, trans. Ross MacKenzie (Edinburgh and London: Oliver and Boyd, Ltd., 1959), 18–33. G. Wingren, *The Living Word: A Theological Study of Preaching and the Church*, trans. Victor C. Pogue (Philadelphia: Fortress Press, 1965), 76; hereafter cited as *LW*. *CL*, 18–22.

4. *CL*, 50–51, 94, 160, 174–75, 185; *LW*, 80–81. G. Wingren, *Gospel and Church*, trans. Ross MacKenzie (Philadelphia: Fortress Press, 1965), 179, 253; hereafter cited as *GC*.

5. *CL*, 90, 162–73, 183, 192–93; *GC*, 114; *LW*, 141, 143; *Theology in Conflict*, 77.

6. *GC*, 100; *LW*, 137. G. Wingren, *The Flight from Creation* (Minneapolis: Aubsburg Press, 1971), 68. Hereafter cited as *FC*.

7. *GC*, 155–56, 165–66; *LW*, 247–49.

8. *LW*, 52 n. 1.

9. *GC*, 71–73.

10. *GC*, 154–55.

11. *FC*, 8.

12. *FC*, 65. G. Wingren, "The Concept of Vocation—Its Basis and Problems," *Lutheran World*, 15, no. 2 (1958), 91–94.

13. *CL*, 137–48; *GC*, 210–14.

14. *CL*, 143, 145; *GC*, 116–17, 137 n. 35.

15. *FC*, 44–52; G. Wingren, "Eschatological Hope and Social Action," *Lutheran World*, 1(1954), 18ff.

16. *LW*, 134 n. 1.

17. Philippians 2:15–18.

18. "The Concept of Vocation," 91–94.

19. *LW*, 31, 49, 204–07.

20. Matthew 25:31–46.

21. K. Vonnegut, *Slaughterhouse Five or The Chidren's Crusade* (New York: Dell Publishing Co., 1969), 93–95.

22. *LW*, 34.

23. *GC*, 165–66.

24. Martin Luther, "Whether Soldiers, Too, Can Be Saved," *Luther's Works*, ed. Jaroslav Pelikan (St. Louis: Concordia Press), vol. 46, pp. 106–07.

Poverty and Power

WILLIAM J. SULLIVAN

Christians are currently enthusiastic about social change, and believe that the poor and oppressed of the world can and should enjoy a better standard of living. Poverty is, like sin, a "scandalous condition." [1] Church leaders and theologians agree that poverty offends the human condition.

Blessed Are The Poor . . .

Gustavo Gutierrez explains that when Christ blessed the poor he indicated their poverty would be eliminated.

> In other words, the elimination of the exploitation and poverty that prevent the poor from being fully human has begun; a Kingdom of justice which goes even beyond what they could have hoped for has begun. They are blessed because the coming of the Kingdom will put an end to poverty by creating a world of brotherhood . . . poverty is an evil and therefore incompatible with the Kingdom of God which has come in its fullness into history and embraces the totality of human existence. [2]

To my knowledge, there are no serious theological objections to Gutierrez's analysis of poverty. None is expected for he only repeats what is a given of current Western Christian thinking, namely, that material poverty is inhuman. The only theological controversy appears to be whether one may use any means at all—even violence—to escape poverty. No one seriously questions whether wealth is better than poverty.

Biblical scholars support systematic theologians in this belief. They agree that Jesus never blessed material poverty, only spiritual poverty. Raymond Brown explains that the poverty Christ blessed is "one that leads men to place their whole trust in God." [3] Such poverty is not and should not be "grinding misery and abject destitution which gives men no time and no energy for anything but bare survival . . . [that] is far from the Christian ideal and should be effaced from the earth." [4] Brown even claims a place "in the spirituality of Matthew's beatitudes . . . for those who are comfortable and wealthy in this world if they preserve a spirit of detachment in relation to their goods, and do not allow their wealth to choke off the vitality of God's word (Matthew 13:22). Nevertheless theirs is not the virtue extolled in Luke's beatitudes." [5]

This language is so familiar that we do not question it. Poverty, even in Luke, is a virtue that is ordinarily within reach only of those who are wealthy and/or powerful enough to practice it. Destitution is not a virtue nor are wealth and power to be avoided. In fact, eminent theologians have with logic and eloquence defended the right of the destitute to strive for wealth and power while Church leaders have encouraged the rich and the powerful to be magnanimous.

There are difficulties with this apparently sensible position. The poverty of Job was certainly grinding misery and destitution, as is the poverty of the world's poor today. Why did Jesus bless poverty so enthusiastically when he apparently was talking about something quite different? Why did the rich young man go away sad when Jesus told him he lacked only one thing? Why did Jesus persist in using language that indicated the poor he blessed were unable to support or defend themselves when he really meant to bless only those who had adequate resources and power to support and defend themselves? Why did Paul describe the incarnation of Jesus in terms of poverty and destitution?[6] Questions such as these remain unanswered in current exegesis. Instead they are avoided by assuming that Jesus would never have been so absurd as to bless grinding misery and destitution. In fact, that state is so far from being a Christian ideal that it should be effaced from the earth although wealth and power may remain.

Revolutionaries also propose the elimination of grinding misery and destitution by forced redistribution of wealth and power. If they are successful, the rich and powerful will become the new class of poor and oppressed. Theologians argue about the morality of revolutionary means but tend to agree with its goals. Thus Jesus is recast as a nineteenth century social reformer and the kingdom of heaven becomes the kingdom of the enlightenment.

Eucharist And Utopia

Visions of fraternity and equality born out of suffering have deep roots in the Christian tradition. The death and resurrection of Christ effected significant change which we experience within the Church, especially in the Eucharist. Current liberation thinkers believe Christian commitment should also be lived within the State. Some even question the integrity of Christian commitment unless oppressive structures are overthrown.

It is my opinion, however, that Christianity is a revolutionary force, but not in the sense described above. Marxism claims to correct society by eliminating what it considers inhuman; Christianity claims to change society by enduring what is inhuman. These two strategies are radically different in their appreciation of the use of power and wealth as well as in their appreciation of the value of poverty and suffering.

Revolutionary movements are commited to unseating or overthrowing the oppressors and assuming their economic wealth and social power. They profess that the problem is the oppressor. Christianity alone, because of its understanding of incarnation and redemptive death, can say the problem is not the current oppressor but rather wealth and power which always incline men to be oppressive. Yet even Christian thinkers have found what Jesus taught about wealth, power, poverty and oppression difficult to understand. Primitive Christian thinkers generally opted to teach that rich and poor complement each other in society. Clement of Rome taught that the rich should support the poor with their alms while the poor not only prayed for them but even thanked God for them.[7] Hermas compared the rich to trailing vines that could bear no good fruit unless they were supported by the poor whom he compared to strong elm trees.[8] Cyprian of Carthage harshly condemned those who had failed the test of persecution. He singled out especially the bishops who had been speculating on real estate in the midst of their peoples' trials. But he blamed the failure of all of the lapsed upon their attachment to their riches. He advised them, now that the persecution was over, to get rid of the wealth that had been their undoing.[9] He even advised parents to give the inheritance of their children to the poor so that their children would benefit from the prayers the poor would offer in gratitude for the assistance.[10]

These Fathers all taught that poverty was a blessed and privileged state. Even so they hesitated to attack wealth and power. Instead they proposed a Christian doctrine in which rich and poor complemented and mutually supported each other. While the rich were preoccupied with their fortunes and thus had little time for prayer, their alms assured them of the prayers of the poor. Cyprian's interpretation of Acts

9:36–39 typified the social awareness of the Fathers of this period: Peter was confident that Tabitha would rise from the dead because so many widows prayed for her. Since these women had been helped by her, their prayers would now be efficacious in bringing her back to life.[11]

Ignatius of Antioch was the most radical of the early Fathers in this regard. He gloried in his chains, looked forward to a martyr's death and even forewarned the Christians at Rome not to intervene should he weaken at the moment of his final test.[12] He warned Christians not to squander all of their resources redeeming slaves for Christians could be slaves and slaves Christians.[13]

Around the year 200, Clement of Alexandria gave the first radically new interpretation of Christ's teaching on power and poverty. He reinstated wealth and power in the Christian Church, explained away the privilege of the poor, and blessed the rich who controlled their passions. He insisted Christ was not concerned about possessions but about passions. His thesis was that the presence or absence of possessions was morally neutral. Men should be neither rewarded nor punished for what they lacked or possessed. He thought it absurd that a man could be rewarded or punished eternally as a result of the amount of wealth and power he had inherited or even earned. Clement's teaching, which he claimed was more worthy of the Savior, was that men were saved or lost because they controlled or failed to control their passions.[14]

This equalized the Christian challenge for both the rich and the poor in a way rich Christians have never questioned since. Some poor people have accepted poverty as a test to be endured without complaint as a condition for gaining eternal salvation. Yet more and more are interpreting it as a curse from which they must be liberated. Christian theologians, with their insights into the condition of the poor and perhaps a sense of guilt, have determined that the only solution is to eliminate oppression and its outward sign poverty by encouraging the redistribution of wealth and power. This solution is not immoral, just unreal. It assumes, as Clement of Alexandria assumed, that the rich can and should be so thoroughly dispassionate about their wealth and power that they will be willing to share it with those who have little or nothing at all.

Problems Of Poverty And Wealth

Neither the national nor the international scene offer any supportive evidence for such an assumption. Half the people in the world now go to bed hungry every night. The same amount of food that is now feeding 210 million Americans would feed 1.5 billion Chinese on an average Chinese diet. While Americans grumble about long lines of cars waiting to get gasoline, the people of India are unable to get enough fuel to run their water pumps or to obtain adequate supplies of nitrate fertilizers. As a result, crops are down while population is increasing.

Henry Pachter, professor of political science at City College of New York and co-editor of *Dissent*, states, "One-third of the world's population, a billion people in Asia and Africa may be undernourished, perhaps starving next year. The boom in raw material prices deprives them of oil, fertilizer and grains." [15] Secretary General Waldheim told a special session of the United Nations General Assembly in April, "The single most devastating indictment of our current world civilization is the continued existence of stark pervasive mass poverty among two-thirds of the world population. It permeates every phase of life in the developing countries in the malnutrition of children, in the outbreaks of diseases, in widespread unemployment, in low literacy rates, in overcrowded cities." [16] And finally, the Sahel, 2.5 million square miles of land, one-fifth of all Africa, is gradually being turned into a sandy wasteland. Estimates put human casualties as high as several hundred thousand, while 20 million head of cattle have also starved.

What is the Christian to make out of this stark fact of poverty? It is little wonder that those Christians who do not identify the poor of the beatitudes with the materially impoverished call for liberation and even revolution. For them, that response is consistent with the gospel and the all-too-evident coexistence of affluence and destitution. But must liberation only be sought from the barrel of a gun? May it not also come upon the arms of a cross?

Poverty as Revolution

The position of Jesus, as reflected by Ignatius of Antioch, is far more revolutionary than current so-called liberation theologies. Philanthropy is not the major thrust of this position. Instead the dangers of wealth are pointed out and there is a hard cynicism about the likelihood of the wealthy using their money or power for the good of the masses. Poverty is the human condition because man is totally dependent upon God the Father, secure only as the birds of the air and lilies of the field. Total dependence upon another is difficult to imagine, much less to practice. Moderation is easier to preach, and generosity in the distribution of wealth and power sounds more reassuring. But history confronts us with a resounding confirmation of the naiveté of that position.

Nor is it solely ancient history which mocks that unreality. In 1973, Kuwait received over $2-billion in oil revenues and offered only $300,000 to assistance programs sponsored by the United Nations. Saudi Arabia collected over $4-billion in oil revenues and contributed nothing to the same programs. One author refers to these and other similar phenomena as "imperialism in reverse." Christians recognize them as common hazards for the rich and powerful. We know of them from Jesus' warnings about the perils of the needle's eye. Inhuman and oppressive existence is much more likely to originate in wealth and power than in their absence.

Biblical authors might have cited the Incarnation as an argument for absolute powerlessness in the face of human existence or as an argument for the philanthropic use of divine power for the good of others. St. Paul argued in Philippians 2:5–11 that Jesus made himself like us in all things, even death. No biblical author, to my knowledge, argues that the rich and the powerful should imitate Jesus in using what they possess for the good of others. The fact is that Jesus gave all for the sake of others and died a felon's death upon the cross.

There is no room in the example of Jesus' life to argue that one may maintain a certain lifestyle in accord with one's state in life, nor that one must put aside a reasonable sum for the needs of the apostolate or the requirements of old age. Such concerns are not evidenced in the life of Jesus. He envisioned the cross or the cup as the baptism he must endure, the price to be paid for being human.

Absolute poverty may also be analyzed as an absolute pre-condition for charity. The poor are unable to defend themselves; they depend totally upon others. Anyone can take advantage of them and many do. Witness the magnitude of the problems confronting abused children, the aged, widows, minority groups within nations as well as nations of the so-called Third and Fourth Worlds. We profess to believe that God loves them; we know men and women use and abuse them. The human response to the vulnerability of the poor is as brutal as the imperial and priestly response to the vulnerability of Jesus.

Christians perceive the problem but, in my judgment, misconceive the solution by their emphasis upon the necessity of even minimal wealth and power. To make the poor and the oppressed wealthy and powerful is simply to create a new caste of oppressors. But even worse, the traditional biblical categories of the poor, i.e., the very young, widows, and foreigners, are most unlikely to profit from any redistribution of wealth and power.

More significant than these practical objections is that Christian love demands the giving of self so that one becomes as vulnerable as the person assisted. Some Christian theorists now seem to suggest that the goal of charity is to make the recipient as invulnerable as the giver.

In the Church, we experience the total vulnerability of the *anawim*, the poor. We die in the baptismal waters and then embrace a new life. We throw off our parental heritage and take up the Christ-life. At the Eucharist we share, as members of the Body of Christ, his flesh and his blood. There are no blacks, no whites, no males, no females, no First, Second, and Third World. We are all one in Jesus Christ. If the same theology applied so facilely to the sacraments were also applied to our tables, our neighborhoods, our businesses, and our schools, the significance of Christianity as revolution would be obvious. As we all share and suffer and endure together, there can be no more rich or poor. We shall all be indigent and vulnerable, or as Jesus suggested, we shall all become like the lilies and the birds.

Notes

1. Gustavo Gutierrez, *A Theology Of Liberation* (Maryknoll, New York: Orbis Books, 1973), p. 299.
2. *Ibid.,* pp. 298–99.
3. Raymond E. Brown, *New Testament Essays* (Milwaukee: Bruce Publishing Company, 1965), p. 270.
4. *Ibid.,* p. 270.
5. *Ibid.*
6. Cf. Philippians 2:5–11.
7. *First Clement,* 38:1, 2.
8. *The Shepherd Of Hermas,* Sim. II, 5.
9. *The Lapsed,* 6.
10. *Treatise VIII,* 18.
11. *Treatise VIII,* 6.

12. *To The Romans,* 2–4.

13. *To Polycarp,* 4:3.

14. *Who Is The Rich Man That Shall Be Saved?,* XI–XII.

15. "Imperialism In Reverse," Henry M. Pachter, *Harper's Magazine,* June 1974, p. 68.

16. *New York Times,* April 10, 1974, p. 12.

Contributors

Elizabeth Bellefontaine, S.C., teaches scripture at Mount Saint Vincent University in Halifax, Nova Scotia.

Leonard J. Biallas is an assistant professor of religious studies at Quincy College in Illinois.

Mary I. Buckley is at St. John's University in New York as an assistant professor in the Department of Theology.

Stephen J. Casey teaches theology at the University of Scranton.

James H. Cone is the author of *Black Theology and Black Power* (1969). He has written extensively on black theology, and teaches at Union Theological Seminary.

Francis P. Fiorenza teaches at the University of Notre Dame, and is on sabbatical during 1974–75 at Union Theological Seminary.

Silvio E. Fittipaldi, O.S.A., is studying the significance of Christian-Buddhist dialog at Temple University. He teaches at Villanova University in the Religious Studies Department.

James Gaffney is a member of the Department of Theology at Illinois Benedictine College in Lisle, Illinois.

Thomas M. McFadden (editor) is chairman of the College Theology Society's publications committee. He teaches at St. Joseph's College in Philadelphia.

Francis J. Reilly is a faculty member at St. Anselm's College in Manchester, New Hampshire.

Letty M. Russell has published *Human Liberation in a Feminist Perspective—a Theology* (1974). She teaches at Yale University Divinity School.

T. Richard Shaull is Professor of Ecumenics at Princeton

Theological Seminary. He has lived in Latin America for a number of years, and has published extensively on the theme of Third-World liberation.

Carl F. Starkloff, S. J., has been long concerned with the relationship between Christianity and American Indian religions. He teaches at Rockhurst College and has recently published *The People of the Center* (1974).

William J. Sullivan teaches within the Department of Religious Studies at St. John Fisher College in Rochester, New York.